Esquire

FATHERS+SONS

Esquire

FATHERS+SONS

11 GREAT WRITERS TALK ABOUT THEIR DADS, THEIR BOYS, AND WHAT IT MEANS TO BE A MAN

EDITED BY DAVID KATZ

HEARST BOOKS
A division of Sterling Publishing Co., Inc.

New York / London
www.sterlingpublishing.com

CONTENTS

ESQUIRE FATHERS & SONS

FOREWORD

No relationship has more power than the one between a father and a son. A man may be closer to his mother, have more impassioned rivalries with his brothers, love his wife more desperately. But father and son—whether for good or ill—that relationship molds a man.

A son sees in his father achievement, mastery—all the things he hopes to be. A father sees in his son potential, the possibility of all the things he has not done and may never do. The relationship is founded on lofty expectations—all the optimism and ambition that define masculinity. And because it is built on expectation, this relationship inevitably has to encounter, and hopefully overcome, disappointment.

Because men fail. At some point, a man will fail his father or a man will fail his son. Whether implicit or explicit, fathers make their sons promises: I will always be there; I will take care of you; I will help you; I will show you how to be a man. Sooner or later, whether by sin of omission or commission, he will break one of those promises. And then the relationship begins to change.

That's where the tension and drama in the following stories come from—the feeling that one person has somehow let the other down, failed to be all that he could have been or was supposed to be. It could be in a small way or in a large way, but when it happens, it teaches a man a lesson as powerful as any in his life.

A son learns a great deal from realizing that his father is flawed, that he is imperfect. Some men never get over the disappointment. Some shrug it off and move forward. Some draw on it for strength, for art, for humor. Each of these scenarios can be found in this collection.

Sooner or later, every man looks in the mirror and sees his father. And whether he is proud to see what he is becoming or whether he is horrified, he once again defines his progress through life by the man who helped give him life.

Sometimes their stories are happy. Sometimes they are sad. But stories of fathers and sons are what define us as men.

David Granger
Editor-in-Chief, *Esquire*

A FEW WORDS FROM
FATHERS

THE BEGINNING

by Daniel Voll

"**B**abies die!" the doctor shouts at me. Our doctor.

I don't want to fight with the doctor who is going to deliver my son. Cecilia is in labor, and we've just gotten to the hospital. It's Friday, 8:00 p.m., New York City. Misty rain outside. "Are *you* going to deliver this baby, Daniel?" he shouts. "Because you're not letting me do my job. You're trying to take over."

Just this morning, Cecilia was standing in front of the mirror breast-feeding a teddy bear. Her due date was a week away, and I still couldn't believe that I was about to be a father. I wanted everything to slow down. I just wanted her to stand naked in front of the mirror a little longer. Now we're in the labor-and-delivery room, and the doctor is yelling at me: "Babies die! Nature is cruel. Not so long ago, babies died routinely. *And* their mothers. I know what's best."

The doctor reaches out to touch Cecilia, but she backs away. He's been her gynecologist since college, but she's angry about this morning's exam. Without Cecilia's consent, he pushed his fingers through her cervix and stripped the membranes. "That *hurts!*" Cecilia yelled out. "You've got to stop!" Sharp contractions began immediately. This procedure, we've just learned, is often done on Friday mornings by doctors who want to get babies out before the weekend.

She whispers in my ear. "I need you to fight for me." All of a sudden, we're deep behind enemy lines. She wants a natural delivery. No C-section. The doctor says she has only a 10 percent chance of that happening. "I know my body," Cecilia says. He claims the baby is overdue. We think he's wrong.

If he wants to cut her open tonight, I tell him, he'll have to cut through me.

We had opted for the benefits of a modern hospital, but all Cecilia wants now is to be left alone. The nurses seem to understand. But what to do about the doctor? "We'll take care of him," one nurse assures us, conspiratorially.

The room where Cecilia will labor and deliver is not such a bad place—wood floors and blond cabinetry. Feels outfitted by Ralph Lauren, except for a large red trash can labeled blood waste. I drag that out into the hall. We dim the overhead lights and put on Mozart. I've brought a boom box, a couple cold bottles of Guinness, a toothbrush, and a change of clothes.

The senior resident, a petite, dark-haired woman, comes in to examine Cecilia. She tells us our doctor is asleep down the hall. "Don't worry, my hands are small," she says. "I won't hurt you."

Cecilia's been having contractions every two minutes all day, but she's only now entering active labor. The resident agrees that Cecilia should go without drugs as long as possible. Contractions will help push the baby down. Drugs will slow progress. But, she warns, the next hours will be painful. She's right.

Cecilia rocks back and forth on the bed, breathing hard. She gets up and leans on walls. Between contractions, she can talk until the next one takes her under. I massage her back. She climbs onto the chair and into my lap.

"Am I snorting like a water buffalo?" she asks.

\ \ \

Cecilia's parents arrive around ten o'clock, smuggling in soup. We're glad to see them. My own father wasn't allowed in the delivery room when I was born. Cecilia's father has never been in a labor-and-delivery room, either. She sees the concern in his face and tries to hide her pain. A few days ago, he and I were drinking pints in an Irish pub and showing off grainy sonogram pictures to the barmaid. Now we both sit at the end of Cecilia's bed. He massages one foot; I massage the other.

Her father tells us they'll be next door in the waiting room, watching the hospital's breast-feeding channel. He says the breast-feeding channel is quite informative. Women with engorged breasts urging their babies to suck. He offers Cecilia breast-feeding tips, and she laughs for the first time all night.

A nurse puts a monitor on Cecilia's belly, and I hear the beep, beep, beep of our son's heartbeat. I watch the glowing red numbers. Now it's 130 per minute; if it drops below 100, he's in distress.

"Please, just pass over me," Cecilia begs the next contraction. She clings to the side of the bed, her knuckles white.

She's tied to the mast.

This goes on for five more hours.

Cecilia's pain threshold is high, and she's strong from years of yoga, but as the contractions intensify, she's astonished. "This is a whole other universe of pain," she says. At three months pregnant, she was in Texas, shooting a documentary on death row. She's danced with Martha Graham, climbed most of the Swiss Alps. Now she can't talk.

Only hand signals.

She wants ice chips.

At 3:00 a.m., I roll up my pants and take Cecilia into the shower. "It will give her relief," the nurse promises, and, although I don't understand why, she's right. Something about ions. For half an hour, I nozzle warm water onto Cecilia's back. Afterward, she vomits.

Her work is paying off. At 4:15, the baby's head is almost in position. Cecilia's been in labor eighteen hours. She finally asks for Demerol to take the edge off. It will slow the contractions, but she needs to rest.

"Danny, don't go to sleep. If you're awake, I'll know everything's going to be OK."

I watch her drift off. I think about my father and how dependent he is on my mother. I have always been afraid to be that helpless. I have never before wanted to be so at the mercy of love. To be a parent, or truly a partner, is to risk being wholly seen. Until now, I have always tried to step back, to leave a margin to move around in, a shadow where I can hide.

I can see the first light outside. The senior resident stops in to say goodbye at the end of her twenty-four-hour shift.

We are handed off to the last of the great combat nurses. Straight out of a MASH unit, she's the nurse I'd hoped for down the stretch. "You're going to have this baby the way you want," she tells Cecilia, sending us back into the shower. "Keep the door locked," she says. "Your doctor is looking for you."

Our doctor strolls in at 9:00 a.m. looking well rested. He says that maybe he was wrong about the C-section. The baby's head is engaged and pressing against Cecilia's cervix. But she needs to dilate six more centimeters before giving birth. That means hours more of severe contractions and pain. He suggests an epidural to numb her from the waist down.

"I want to be able to feel when it's time to push," Cecilia says.

"You will," the nurse promises.

We vote for the epidural.

But the anesthesiologist can't get the damn needle into her back. I watch it bend. He tries again, two vertebrae lower. Finally, he gets it right.

Cecilia is fully dilated at 1:00 p.m. The room is buzzing. The nurse flips the surgical light on. The blood waste can returns.

Our doctor, in scrubs and a hairnet, looks like a guy behind the counter at Burger King. Cecilia is on her back. Time to push! Time to bring our son into the world! Wait—one last thing. Cecilia wants the Rolling Stones, loud: *Pleased to meet you, hope you guess my name* . . .

Deep breath . . . Now *push* . . . Quick breath . . . *push* . . . Quick breath . . . *push* . . . Now rest. This goes on for an hour.

The doctor picks up a pair of scissors. *Scissors.* Shiny scissors. Damn, an episiotomy. He wants to cut her perineum to help bring out the baby. Cecilia doesn't want this; she'd rather risk a small tear. She's told him this a hundred times. "Prepare the local," he tells the nurse. She ignores him. Gives me a wink. No question who's in charge here. He protests, and she raises a hand: "We're going to give her a chance."

He puts down the scissors.

With the next contraction, the nurse and I help Cecilia squat on the bed. Now gravity is working with her.

"I feel him coming," Cecilia yelps. Five pushes later, his head crowns—dark, wet hair, a pale scalp. "Look into the doctor's glasses," the nurse tells Cecilia. "You can see him coming out." She gives a final push, and now our son's head bursts out, facedown, into the doctor's hands. He sucks a breath, hungry for air. His body emerges, but his skin looks gray, like death, and I have a moment of genuine panic. But with every breath, his skin will pinken.

2:19 p.m. Twenty-eight hours since Cecilia felt the first contraction. And now he is on her chest, his tiny hands reaching toward her face.

Her arms around him. His eyes are huge and slate blue.

I want to thank the doctor, but I can't talk. He seems amazed him-self—no stitches, no cuts. Cecilia looks more beautiful than ever. The baby is nursing at her breast. Cecilia's father pours champagne. "A toast," he says, lifting his Styrofoam cup. "To this wonderful boy, a long life, a healthy one, an interesting one, an adventurous one. On the cusp of the new century, we toast this wonderful Harper."

Tonight, Cecilia and I will sleep together in the narrow hospital bed, the baby on my chest: seven pounds seven ounces, the weight of my entire world.

THE BABYPROOFER

by Larry Doyle

We got our babyproofer through a friend, who came to visit after the baby was born and had a cow. There are so many dead babies in this house, she said, her fingers fluttering about. The wife got pretty upset, but this friend—really more my wife's friend—caressed her head, blotted her cheeks, and said the important thing was that our baby wasn't dead yet and there was still a chance we could stop the baby before he killed himself.

The babyproofer cost seventy-five dollars an hour.

There's a dead baby, he said, not a foot in the door, re the staircase. Then in a bouncing gesture along the baseboard: Dead baby, dead baby, dead baby . . . What is that?

What, that penny?

Dead baby.

Our poor baby died so many times during that initial consultation: 187, according to the babyproofer's written assessment; it seemed like more. Dead baby in the toilet. Dead baby down the disposal. Dead baby with my scissors plunged into his carotid artery.

The babyproofer turned to me at one point. Just curious, did you want to have this baby?

The babyproofer needed a ten-thousand-dollar retainer.

For that kind of money, I said, just trying to lighten the mood a little, we could buy a whole new baby.

The wife did not laugh; the babyproofer stood up.

I haven't lost a baby yet, he said. But who knows, maybe I am a little overcautious. Why don't you just buy one of those babyproofing books? They only cost about twenty bucks.

The babyproofer went through the initial ten grand rather quickly. In fairness, a lot of it was materials: thirty-four ceramic outlet guards at $19.95 each (the plastic ones, my wife agreed, weren't darling, and they leached a substance that caused fatty tumors in cancer-prone mice); sixty-two baby gates at $39.95; four safes (pharmaceuticals, soaps, and bath products; cleaning supplies; cooking and eating utensils; and assorted swallowables) at $195. The Cuisinatal Food Reprocessor alone cost $3,000, but it does puree at twice the FDA's shockingly lax standards and can strain out some of your larger, more harmful bacteria. There was some debate in our house whether we really needed six baby dummies (at $699 per!), but I suppose the wife is right—if even one of them is stolen, it's probably worth it.

Beyond the money, we've had to make a lot of adjustments to create what the babyproofer calls a survival-friendly environment. Some of it makes sense, like not allowing anyone who has been to Africa, Southeast Asia, or Mexico into the house. But the hospital scrub-down before every diaper change seems excessive; it's so heart-wrenching with the baby crying the whole time. And I do miss TV, though not enough to risk coming home one day to find my lazy, violent, obese baby with a television set toppled on his head.

The thing I hated most was getting rid of the dog, but what could I do? It kept tasting the baby.

I haven't been sleeping much. I sit up in bed, worrying about all the money we've spent but also whether we've spent enough. I go through each of the 187 dead babies in my head, running their fatal scenarios against the prophylactic measures we've taken. Did I remember to spin the combination on the toilet? Did I stare at the bedside monitor, waiting for the baby to flatline, which he does five or six times a night? So far, it's just been that he's pulled off his wires, but running in there five or six times a night and fumbling around for those shock paddles, it takes something out of you.

My wife and the babyproofer are driving up to Ojai for a weekend seminar on antioxidant baby massage at some resort. I forget exactly why they can't take the baby; the spa supplies its own practice infants for insurance reasons, maybe.

So here I am, left holding the baby.

He is so beautiful. I want to lift the polarized visor of his helmet to get a better look; I want to kiss his cheeks, his nose, his forehead—damn the salmonella. But I can't. I know that. I rock the baby gently, in no more than a twenty degree arc, no more than twenty oscillations per minute, whispering in the five-to-ten-decibel range, Please don't die, baby. Please don't die. Not on my shift.

SAM

by Alec Wilkinson

ROMANCE

My father held himself aloof from our family in a way that was common for the period, the 1950s and '60s. We lived in the suburbs of New York City, and he had a job in Manhattan; he was the art director of the magazine *Woman's Day*. He was a charming, bluff, and somewhat insensitive man, and he was a philanderer, too, so a part of his attention was always somewhere other than in his household. I held him, though, in high regard, as children tend to do, and imitated his example, which was only intermittently appropriate, and so I had a lot of flawed experiences, and when enough of them had piled up, I sat in a leather chair in the office of a Jungian analyst once or twice a week for a number of years and, staring just to the left or right of him or at the row of small fetishes on the bookcase above his head, described my difficulties with my mother, while he replied, "I think you have more issues with your father." Son of a bitch isn't even listening to me, I thought, until I had a dream in which I was a teenager about to take the ice in a hockey game and discovered that my father had put me in skates with broken blades. After that, I began to carry him a little bit less glamorously in my mind and eventually some kind of balance within me shifted, and somewhat unexpectedly and a little bit late—I was forty-two—I arrived at a point where I felt that I was prepared to raise a child. Prepared, in the sense that I imagine the poor holy loser who died in the bus in Alaska felt that he was prepared, with his rifle, his books, and his bag of rice, to wait out the weather.

Before we leave Confession Gulch, I would like to add that I have been married twice. The first time, my wife and I both picked wrong and the marriage ended sadly after seven years. In truth, it had been over for some time, so it also took a few sessions in the leather chair to see why I had made such a piece of bad judgment, why both of us had engaged in it, and what I could do to make sure I would marry again—happily, if I was lucky. When I did, I used sometimes to wake in the middle of the night and think, Please, God, let me live out my natural life in the company of this woman I love. My son was born six years ago, and it is not that my feelings for my wife ever changed, except to deepen, but I was aware that when he had been in the world only a short time, I had begun thinking, Please, God, let me live to see as much of his life as I can.

What has followed between us could not truly be described as a love affair, unless your version of one includes tests and dismissals and reversals and forbearance and an awareness that whatever you had thought the affair might be, had hoped or imagined it might be, is precisely what it won't, or even can't (apparently), ever be.

WATERWORKS

I did not expect to cry when my son was born—it seemed a silly and conventional and trivial thing to do, weep for joy, like a figure in an advertisement—but I did, quite suddenly and without warning, as if it were a reflex. He was delivered in the morning by a midwife in a hospital in Manhattan, and I felt embarrassed, slightly, to be weeping among women, to be weeping when no one else was, as if trying to emphasize that the strength and capacity to bear pain that my wife had demonstrated were laudable, but I was *sensitive*, so I looked toward the floor and wiped away the tears. When his face had appeared, I had seen his eyes, and the instant in which consciousness lit them. He was examined briefly by a doctor and then lay with his mother, and I watched them for a while, then went to get some coffee and bagels for our breakfast. When I got back, Sara, my wife, was in her room with Sam, our son, wrapped up—a small bundle with a cap on, a face about the size of a softball—and she handed him to me, and I held him for the first time. He felt like a piece of china in my hands. I held him the way you would hold a fragile and tiny creature whose existence depended entirely on the lightness of your touch. There was a nurse with us in the room. She said, "You'll scare him if you don't hold him tighter. They need to know they're being supported."

I spoke his name. I looked into his eyes, which had the luminance of polished stone. What I felt mainly was the absence of what I expected to feel—that is, I thought his arriving in my arms would somehow stimulate an awareness I had never felt toward anything before, a resonance that was primitive and universal and private, a code shared between us that couldn't possibly be stirred by any other form of contact, the kind of experience that would appear in a movie. Instead I heard a voice in my mind saying things such as, This is *my* son—*my son*. Yes, this is *my son*. And at the same time asking, Shouldn't something else, something more, be happening? Pay closer attention.

I have never asked any other man if he had an experience such as mine, but I don't think mine is singular. How could it be? I can imagine men holding their son or daughter for the first time and having feelings regarding the child's destiny or place in the family and among his or her ancestors or the traits he or she appears to display, but such feelings are sentimental, and sentimental feelings are a lie concocted to cover the feelings you might more straightforwardly have. You hate your brother who tormented you, but persist in feeling that your up-bringing with him as your comrade and sergeant at arms was fortu-nate; it made you tougher. I am capable of insensitivity, as my father was, but I am not an insensitive person. I would mistrust the account of any man who told me that the first time he held his child he felt profoundly attached to him. Attached to what, really? Someone you're meeting for the first time, who is incapable of returning your feelings, who has only a peripheral awareness of you and none really of who you are, or of his relation to you, or that you might intend for him or her to be a fireman as you have been or a union man or a doctor or preside over a commercial empire or replace Wayne Gretzky or Wil-lie Mays or James Taylor or John Coltrane or Billie Holiday? I do not mean that the moment of first embrace is not significantly charged, only that its import is elusive, and the elusiveness is the first signal that the process of caring for a child is fraught with ambiguity and things you can't know. A child is a territory, a landscape, a region, an outpost, a republic and island of worry.

ILLUSION

You forget a lot of it. The first year is hell, I remember that. You don't sleep. The fatigue accumulates. Your child goes to bed, you have a little bit of fun, then you realize he has a two-hour head start on you. You see in your wife's face a concern, a preoccupation even, that you never saw before. The carefree look is gone, anyway. The emotional balance of your household is altered. Your wife and child have formed an alliance that at times excludes you. They spend so much time to-gether and are so intimate with each other that it was bound to hap-pen. My sense of my son as an enigma was reinforced during the first year because there was little I could provide for him. So far as I could tell, he liked dimly lit rooms, tranquil surroundings, breast milk, and

the company of his mother. Because I had read about studies conclud-
ing that an infant prefers to his father's voice the higher, softer tones
of his mother's speech, I tried for a while talking to Sam in a womanly
voice, then worried that I had confused him in some essential way
about the properties of masculine life, so went back to my own voice,
to which he seemed only occasionally to respond. Sometimes he appeared to enjoy himself when I whistled.

A child's personality hardly emerges before he is seven or eight
months old. During most of his or her first year, what you are aware of
really is the child's temperament: his capacity for frustration, whether
he is cautious or extends himself toward the world. It is easy to imagine
who he is—that is, to make up an identity for him, as if he were a screen
on which to display the images you have always intended for your son
or daughter—and to persuade yourself that he or she is moving toward
becoming some version of those images, and to do it all without really
even being aware of it, to think that really you are occupied simply with
his development, with his becoming, say, someone who will be accomplished at math because you played Mozart for him as he lay in his crib,
overlooking that probably what you were doing was making it difficult
for him to sleep, overstimulating him, making him nervous, and depriv-
ing him of rest. You meant well, and you can tell him that thirty years
down the road when he confronts you, although it is very difficult to
know what will prey on the minds of the adults who are small children
now—certainly not what bothered us; it was a different time, the fifties
and sixties and seventies, and people behaved differently and felt differently about what was proper in the way of raising a child. In any case,
the slow appearance of his character has perhaps to do with the design
of childhood. (Certainly in the past, and in cultures where women were
not sufficiently valued and babies were killed for being of the wrong sex,
a boy who disappointed his father might also be left in the forest.) So

they emerge slowly. You become attached to them and to your version of them, and then they begin perilously to become themselves, someone different from your idea. This calls for a great deal of restraint, to let a child develop according to his nature. To give him sufficient guidance that he becomes equipped with the virtues and judgment he needs to preserve himself and to flourish but not so much that you cause him to repress parts of himself out of fear that they will not be accepted.

Children are utterly dependent. If they meet with disapproval, they will assume that something is wrong with them. Their security, their lives, depend on keeping their mothers and fathers interested in them. If a mom is taken with the bottle or drugs, or the dad is emotionally withdrawn or hostile to the child's well-being, the child will build an explanation for why he has brought such an existence on himself. The alternative—mother or father is unreliable—is a story by Stephen King, your well-being in the hands of people who are capricious about your welfare, who have their own plans for your future, who reward you for certain behavior that might make you uncomfortable and punish you for behavior you find fulfilling. Making a mess, for example.

We are only a few generations removed from the Victorian idea of the child as a little adult, which gave way to the child as a small being with instincts for sex, a devious and slothful package, which gave way to the child as a being engaged in behaviors and activities designed for his pleasure to oppose and thwart the interests of his parents, one who needs to be subdued, to be broken the way a horse might require it—spare the rod and spoil the child, and the advice current in my parents' generation of letting a child put down for the night lie in his crib crying; if you pick him up you'll only give him the impression that the world is a compassionate place interested in seeing him protected. Then he'll manipulate you mercilessly the rest of your life.

EVANESCENCE

My wife and I haven't been to a movie since my son was born, in 1993. I have seen movies on airplanes and I have rented them, but none longer than an hour and a half, because that would keep us up too late. A year ago, I walked past a restaurant on Broadway that has a big window facing the street and saw the people at the tables, and in the instant before my mind focused, I thought, So how does that work, you go in there and ask for food and they prepare it and you pay them; how do you know what you can ask for?

Before I had a child, I had no interest in children; I had thought it was possible I might never have one. I didn't think children were amusing, sometimes I thought they were scary, and I was always on the side of the people on the airplane who crane their necks to stare at the mother unable to calm her child's crying.

I was not aware before Sam was born of the circumstance of feeling hostage to the unfolding of the universe, to the things that lie in wait for your child, the torments and hardships and assaults. I now know that there are disasters lurking everywhere for a child, many of them simple and commonplace. The threat of dehydration for the infant who throws up for too long—a day without water is all it seems to take—so that his eyes may roll back into his head, even while you are waiting in the doctor's anteroom, and you will have to be rushed to the hospital, carrying your child in your arms with people ahead of you kicking doors open, as on TV. Then the children's ward and children walking around with eyes that seem to have no light in them.

I am convinced that one needs to live beside one's children with the feeling that they might not be there at the end of the day, or that you won't, or your wife won't. There are accidents and illnesses, there are divorces. The cemetery is always waiting.

A DISCLAIMER

I should probably announce that I have an eccentric child and that his eccentricities have influenced my feelings about childhood and being a father. What afflicts him, his mother and I only partly know. He appears, from tests and the opinions of various people with diplomas on their walls, to have great difficulty with sensations. Sounds are too loud, touch is often too abrasive or hard or ticklish or startling, something impedes his speech, he has no peripheral vision, and he has trouble organizing the elements of visual images—photographs and paintings and the movements on a television screen. I am not sure exactly how he views images, but it puts me in mind of the natives of whatever territory it was who were shown photographs of their faces and saw in them only areas of black and white.

My son began crawling when he was supposed to, but he dragged one leg. The world, though, has an abundance of people who tell you when your child has trouble, say, speaking, that their great-uncle so-and-so didn't say a word until he was four and then he framed perfect sentences, or in our case they say, "Did you ever meet anyone who didn't learn how to walk?" so you think, Well, that's unusual, the leg dragging, but they're right, and there isn't much you can do with the diagnosis of a child that young anyway, unless the difficulties are severe. So my son has grown into a radiant child who is a little clumsy and has a list of experiences he can't tolerate. My friend William Maxwell, the novelist, says, "Don't worry about him, he has the soul of a poet." Like a lot of poets, then, he isn't much socialized, because his excitement at the appearance of other children overrides what social patterns he might have collected by observing the way other children act, and instead of restraining himself, he races up to them and stands too close and waves his arms while he talks loudly, and this scares them. Some children it doesn't bother at all, but the majority don't cotton to it. Moreover, he doesn't have an older brother or sister whose manners he can imitate. If your attention is distracted by the imminence and immensity of the world and its lights and textures and sounds, if you are constantly alert to voices from the other side of the room or the movements of other children and adults in order to assess whether they contain some threat to you and so that you can keep some distance between yourself and them, your mind is occupied and hasn't got time to address the muscular patterns necessary for speech or movements. You fall behind. And once you are behind, what is measured is how far behind you are and whether you have fallen so far behind that you might not catch up. If you are a five-year-old with the capacities of a four-year-old, do you become a twenty-year-old with the capacities of a sixteen-year-old, or does the equation change? No one knows.

If you are father or mother to such a child, you might think that you have been wronged. You might, as I have occasionally done, feel resentful of the simple commonness, the uncomplicatedness, on display in the lives of garden-variety children, and then something, the sight in the newspaper of a child separated from his parents in Kosovo, say, might cause you to reflect that if this is the worst thing that happens to you and your child, among the catalog of grievances and disappointments and tragedies and unfair happenings in life, you will be lucky and you should probably shut up about it so that the Almighty doesn't hear you and send something else your way with the note, *You thought that was bad.*

A child such as my wife and I have needs extra care. You know what he doesn't like—loud places, places where there is a great deal of activity, especially chaotic places, especially loud, chaotic places—and you avoid taking him to any such places. You try to give him what he likes. The seashore, the wide-open beach, with no avenues of ambush for any adversary, with room for everyone, with the sounds of the waves and the games of running from them and into them and having them tumble you over and the dunes to climb and the sand to dig tunnels in and build cities on that you can destroy. You try to make him happy, to make his life, since it includes so much torment, a pleasure. The longer I can make him happy, the better I feel. The world with its thousand and one things is always waiting there to disappoint him, to bruise his feelings, to exclude him, and I figure that the more capital my wife and I give him in the form of solid fun, the more likely he is to spin off from the distasteful experience into another that pleases him and not to become stuck brooding on the insufficiencies that have made him a figure of sport or rejection for the moment.

One important thing a parent can do for a child, I think, is provide him with a sense of safety.

IRONY

An irony of raising such children is that, if you are like me, you spend your life trying to get away from the small-minded and conventional people, the gym teachers and guidance counselors and spinster penmanship instructors who have a hold over you when you are young, and finally you're shed of them and then you have a child and they get their claws into you all over again. In order to obtain from the state the money to help pay for a portion of some of the therapies my son receives, he had to submit to examinations conducted by people who work for the government. The most indignant I have ever been made as an adult was when I learned that one of them, a psychologist, had asked my son, my heartbeat, my household angel, who was then four, "Have you ever wanted to kill yourself? Have you ever wanted to kill anyone else?"

Then it becomes time to get your child into school, which, if you intend it to be a private school, is not simple. When we went for an interview at one school, a woman with a clipboard said, "Is yours the child who also speaks Russian?" No three-year-old speaks Russian as a second language, a few words of Russian, some phrases perhaps, but a couple desperate enough to place their child had had the nerve to describe their three-year-old as a speaker of a complicated foreign language. I wasn't so surprised at that; people are always willing to make fools of themselves. What surprised me was that, so far as I could tell, the school had taken them seriously.

Schools do not like an eccentric or lively child. Schools—any school, a public school, the most prestigious private school, the school with the reputation for having great concern for the inner life of the child—are all interested in the same thing: tractability. None of them want a child who does not do what he is told. It is nice if your three-year-old plays the cello or speaks Hebrew or can ride a horse, but if he can't perform according to commands, if he is willful or resistant, you will have difficulty placing him in the school you might most wish he would attend, unless of course you are fortunate enough to have sound public schools in your neighborhood. Such a child makes the lives of everyone involved, the teachers and the administrators, more difficult. Other parents resent an obstreperous child. A child who is aggressive. During the interviews of three-year-olds, which are enveloped in mystery, only one assessment is taking place. Absent the variables of whether yours is a child of minority parents or not, prosperous or not, absent the consideration of how many spaces are available for siblings and boys and girls, only one judgment is taking place, indeed only one is possible, since the range of behaviors for children that age is so limited. Your child arrives and plays with two or three other children, then, having been told to, he puts the toys away and sits down for juice and a cookie, perhaps while a story is read. If your child plays nicely, fine, that's nice, nice child. The only gesture that matters is whether, when he is instructed to, he puts away the toys and sits down with the others. If he decides that he is having fun playing with the toys and wants to continue and resists, if he cries in frustration, he has failed his interview and has no chance of being accepted. He has displayed what the school will regard as difficulty with transitions, or, in the language of bureaucracy, he will be said to have difficulty transitioning. They will thank you for coming, and you will receive in the mail a letter saying that the school is disappointed not to be able to admit your child but that there were an unusual number of siblings this year. His future at that school is likely hopeless, unless you are in the position to make a donation of astonishing proportions.

ANOTHER IRONY

For a couple of years, before I knew anything in my son was compromised, I thought that he was more interesting than the boys I saw in his classroom, more able to concentrate, more diverse in his reactions to play, more inventive, and more avid in his joy. The other boys seemed ordinary, a little mean, a little sneaky, a little quick to gang up and exclude, a little taken with aggression. The first time I began to feel something was amiss with Sam, I was watching him in his classroom and noticed that when he was moved toward an aggressive gesture, when another boy, say, had taken a toy he was playing with, Sam tried to get the toy back. There was a struggle. Once the matter was handled, he let it drop. If he had a conflict, he pushed or pulled in plain view. The other boys, I noticed, usually waited until the teachers were looking the other way and pushed or pinched or slapped the other child and impersonated innocence when the teacher looked in their direction. This, I thought, was cowardly. Because my son was open in his behavior, he was more often caught at it. I told one of the teachers that I was proud of him for not misbehaving behind their backs, that the other boys often struck me as angry and mean-spirited and were rarely brought to account because they were sneaky about it. The teacher was nearly as fond of Sam as I was. It pained her to say, "Yes, and you wonder why they have learned not to get caught and Sam hasn't."

My son's difficulties make simple coordination a problem for him. He could not ride a tricycle as a toddler because he could not alternate the actions of his feet without thinking about it. Among my own meager accomplishments are the kind of tennis game and skating style you can have only if you began these activities very early in life and practiced them intensely, so I had imagined that my son and I would go skating together and play tennis, but his difficulty controlling his excitement, which gives him at tranquil times the air of an ecstatic, means that he can't really yet concentrate on an activity as intricate as a tennis swing, or as relaying to his brain the myriad signals involved in maintaining your balance on ice skates. He is a terrific climber, and although he often looks as if he is about to lose his balance, he never does. I was pleased to realize that I would not likely be spending his adolescence in a car traveling between Providence and Boston and Philadelphia to take him to hockey tournaments, but I was concerned that he would not have the protective coloration of an athlete—being accomplished at tennis and captain of the hockey team had gotten me a lot of free passes.

I have no interest in being the kind of parent whose child takes lessons at cello and horseback riding and French and modern dance. Too great an involvement in these activities suggests parents who are social climbers or who have too little time to spend with their children. What I didn't realize was that there is an alternative version of this circuit of activities in which you have a child who takes speech therapy twice a week and has occupational therapy on the other three days.

A PLAN FOR THE FUTURE

Children are made uncomfortable by eccentricity, because it suggests mysteries they know intuitively they are not equal to. They will set upon children who are sufficiently different from them, or who seem to be made for their sport, to cause them anxiety. I have no idea how my son will do as an adolescent, whether he will escape harassment or be the object of it, but if he is a target of it, I will tell him to try to find ways to avoid the person who bullies him, or to talk his way out of a confrontation, to outsmart his adversaries and leave them looking for easier marks. If he is unable to do one of these things, or if the schoolyard constantly throws him and the bully together, if the bully can't be escaped and he is making my son unhappy, I might also try to tell my son that the world is not built for our happiness and that we have to accommodate some degree of misery and ride it out the best we can.

If I feel that the bully might harm my son, I plan to visit the bully. I will pretend to be interested in something he is engaged in, perhaps. I am Sam's father, I might say. How are you? Those are terrific arms you have, you must lift weights, wonderful. Listen, are you busy, could we go sit over on that bench and talk for a moment? All right, here's fine, sure, listen, what I have to say is, I understand from Sam that you make him unhappy, you seem to like to tease him, and I just wanted to suggest that you find someone else, would that be hard? A little? All right, that's fair. Well, here's what I'm thinking: I'm thinking, if you don't quit, I will find you somewhere, when you really aren't thinking about me or Sam, of course, and I or someone representing my interests will beat you within an inch of your miserable, worthless little life, you understand? One more time I hear from Sam that he had any trouble from you of any kind, and those are the consequences for you. Everything in your life at one moment will be as good as it ever has been, and the next moment you will wake up in a hospital room, with double vision and your head hurting and you unable to take solid food. If you think I am not serious about this, try me. Go ahead, tell your father.

When the father calls me, I will say that his son, who makes things up, might need psychiatric help. If you think that this behavior is discreditable of me, I would suggest that we are all immortal in our souls, not in our characters.

LOVE

The physical pleasure, the intimacy, the smell of their hair, their bodies, their closeness, their acceptance of you as their sheltering presence, the way they look when they sleep, their breathing in the night, the light in their eyes, is intoxicating to the point of exquisiteness. Throughout my son's life I have now and then thought of him as a household divinity—that is, as an uncorrupted presence of joy. Like any idol, he is susceptible to vanity and solipsistic behavior, he is interested in his acceptance as a majestic being, jealous and intolerant of the attention of his subjects being divided. Sometimes he hurts me so deeply by what appears to be indifference that I think I will refuse to look at him for the rest of his life, I will give him up. I hope that he will have none of my smaller and undesirable qualities and all of my better ones. I want him to grow into a man who is unplagued, regarded affectionately for his sensitivity and intelligence and candor and steadfastness and a tranquility at the heart of his being that comes from knowing that he has been loved, that he has no obligation to carry forth a family myth, that he is unencumbered. And that he will value the company of his mother and father because he feels it is uncomplicated by our insistence that he abandon his identity for one we need him to embrace.

Perhaps nearly every observation I've made could be wrong or applies only in my case. I know one thing: A moment arrives when your child leaves your lap and you realize he isn't coming back.

THE LOST BOYS

by Tom Chiarella

There's a room in my house with a television, a computer, a chair, and a couch in it and not much more. A room in which nothing matches the blue paint my ex-wife and I chose almost a decade ago. We split six years later. I never bothered to change the paint. There's a bookshelf full of board games and an Xbox on the floor. My sons call it the Halo room.

They call it that because all we do in there is play Halo, a multiplayer combat game for Xbox. My two boys. Their friends. Me. Sometimes one, sometimes four, sometimes eight of us, lolling on the carpet, chopping the air in front of us with game controllers, the afternoon sun falling in dusty chunks of color on the ratty carpet. If one of us is on the phone, then the other two are playing Halo. If one of us is on the computer, then the other two are playing Halo, a game in which one heavily armed futuristic soldier runs loose on a space station trying to kill other equally well armed futuristic soldiers, aliens, and mutants. We once agreed on an hour a day, maximum, but it's not out of the question for us to play four or seven hours, to order pizza, to sit there and bet pennies on the number of kills we get. There is frequent yelling and cursing. I run tournaments with their friends in which I place odds like an old-time bookie eyeballing the horses at distant tracks.

And I know, in some fashion, I am doing wrong by them, indulging them, letting them stay at this, deep in this dumb game. Someone ought to get them outside, get them talking about something else. But I always figure at least we're in there together, into something, learning something. And there are no drugs nearby.

Early last summer my fourteen-year-old, Gus, saw a show on MTV called *True Life: I'm a Gamer*, and for a while that was the buzz while we played. The show featured a guy who could play Pac-Man perfectly and a PC gamer who was unbeatable, who made a living by playing. Most notable to my son was this house full of young men somewhere who did nothing but play video games all the time, guys who lived with only guys, who went by the names they recorded in the high-score areas of video games.

These guys, he told me, were all pulled together in a group called, adolescently, the Order of Light. They had a Web site. As the show went into reruns, my sons and their friends watched it again and again. They jabbered about the Order of Light as they knocked me over with rifle butts and shot me with sniper rifles and otherwise fragged me in Halo. "We should have an order," my ten-year-old, Walter, said. "We should set up rules for the way we do things."

"We are a family," I said. "We do have rules."

"It's not the same," he shrugged. "Dad, those guys have dog tags. They're like the Army."

One afternoon, there were five of us in the Halo room, killing one another with remarkable alacrity, when I started to wonder just how good my sons really were. I was willing to accept that they were better than me and that the game required a sort of athletic sensibility that they appeared to have in spades. I am forty-two years old, gainfully employed. But unlike other parents, who play a video game for a minute or two to placate their child, then go off to pay bills, I play to beat them. I want to kill my sons. But no matter how much I worked at it, I was, like most adults, an incredibly weak player, and they got bored playing with me. It frustrated me that I could practice for a week, read Web sites, map and remap the layout of key areas, only to have them come back from their mom's and beat me even worse.

Then again, maybe they were simply brilliant. So I asked them, "Who do you think the best player in the world is?"

Gus didn't hesitate, speaking in that way kids do when they're gaming, intent upon the screen, not looking up, pressing down, manipulating the space in front of him: "Suicide Bob."

"Yep," Walter said, reloading.

The others who had seen the show piped in: "No doubt."

"How much better could he be than you?" I asked. I could not imagine better intuition or faster reactions than those of my older son, who seemed to be able to sneak up on me in any room in the game and dispatch me with the cool indifference of a dogcatcher. I figured we must be at the top end. Or at least my sons were.

"Way better," they said. "He's the best."

"He's like Marshall Faulk," Walter said.

"He's like the president of Halo," said one of his friends. "Like George Bush." They laughed.

"More like Sammy Soso," Gus said. Not one of them was looking at me. Nor was I looking at them. We were watching the screen, where Gus was hiding behind a concrete column with a rocket launcher at the ready.

"Sosa," I said.

"Whatever."

I told them I wanted them to play against this Suicide Bob. Show me his Web site. I promised that if they wrote and made contact, I'd use our vacation time to go down there to see how badass these guys really were.

And with that, we began to train.

There are rooms like ours all over the country, wired and rewired, boxes tied to boxes tied to controllers and phone lines, televisions clumped in at various angles, shades drawn. There isn't much poetry in places like these. They are rooms that look, at all times, as if the world had just stood up and run out to get burgers. It is the province of men and boys left to their own devices. Dorm rooms. Game rooms. Television rooms. Dens. Ours seems sort of cozy, in the way day-old clothes are inviting; you could just climb right in at any time. Coke cans pile up at either end of the couch, generally a couch that's slipping its way toward a landfill day by day.

As the year drew out, we spent more time there, with more of their friends. The circle grew. We concentrated on one setting of Halo, working to master one set of weapons and talking constantly to one another about everything we had learned. We were on a quest. Now the boys were willing to teach me.

"Fire while you're running," Walter said. "Don't always hide. Don't be so afraid."

"You have to understand the whole room," Gus said. "Not just what's in front of you."

I got better the way a jogger gets better, a few steps every day, a few seconds a week. I had always figured one of my sons could beat these guys once. Now maybe even I had a chance, on this one setting, in this one world, with just the one weapon. It was like learning to play one song really well on the guitar. I figured I had a chance to sit in with the band.

When I told my friends that I was taking the boys to meet the Order of Light, they seemed puzzled or alarmed. They punched out questions in little jabs, like television cops: "Memphis? Video gamers? Why?" Like most people, they sensed trouble. Lots and lots of trouble. Trouble right here in this country. With a capital *T*, and that rhymes with *V*, and that stands for *video games*. Most assumed video games to be pointless, antisocial, and even bad for the economy.

They saw our quest as pointless, too. "I'm taking them to see their heroes," I said to one friend.

"Guys playing video games?" she said. "Some heroes."

But you have to pick your own heroes. My boys had already done that. We were going to see them.

We drove, and it is one ass-bad, bone-tiring haul from Indiana, where I live, to Memphis along the Mississippi when you're in a Buick with two boys listening to Walkmans through the dreary flatness of southern Illinois, Missouri, Arkansas. By comparison, Memphis looks like a city on the hill.

I talk to Suicide Bob on my cell phone from the interstate. He gives me the pass code to the gate of his apartment complex. When I punch it in, Walter says, "Just like a game." Past the fence sits a massive oval of asphalt with a menagerie of cars knocked into every parking space. It feels tight and dangerous, not fencing people out so much as keeping them in. Men sit on the hoods of the cars, watching us as if we were, well, aliens on a spaceship. More gaming. Even now.

We ring the bell of the third-floor walk-up, and a kid answers the door—or a man. It's hard to say. He stands up on his toes and bounces, in sore need of a haircut and a shower. He's very white, the kind of kid who rides by you on a bike without drawing notice. He might have delivered my last pizza. This would be Suicide Bob.

Two others are there—a guy who calls himself Longshot and the weirdly named Ryuji Sakata, equally white, equally wan. Polite beyond reproach. They shake hands the way kids do, as if I were making them kiss or something. The main television, high definition, sits dead center in the living room, as huge and clear as a mirror. They are gaming. Virtua Fighter. They have, they tell me, just been robbed. Do I want a Coke?

The whole place is rigged and networked with the kind of inventory a thirteen-year-old dreams of: eight televisions, four personal computers, one TiVo, three Xboxes, two GameCubes, two Dreamcasts, two PlayStations, two PlayStation 2's, one PlayStation 2 equipped for Japanese games, two Neo-Geos, one Neo-Geo Pocket, two Wonder-Swans, one TurboExpress, a Game Boy Pocket, a Game Boy Color, a Game Boy Advanced, a Game Boy Advanced SP, twenty-eight controllers, and 762 video games. Probably six hundred feet of cable runs across the floors of all four rooms. Every surface of every piece of furniture, save the couch and recliner, is covered in wires, game boxes, and hardware. In the kitchen, the only recognizable utensils are a box of fast-food straws and a glass of plastic forks. The fridge is full of Cokes. Not Diet Cokes. Not Dr. Peppers. Cans and cans of bright red Cokes. Sticky-sweet Coke. Like eighty of them.

The guys are ready to play, having taken the day off work. We all sit. Me, the old man, on the couch. Them—the boys, all of them—on everything and anything, the arms of chairs, the floor, cardboard boxes. My children fold in among these strangers as if they've known them all their lives. Within minutes, we start gaming.

For the next several hours, they pour into the apartment, members of the Order, stopping by one by one: D, the hack-and-slash gamer (who works in document sorting at FedEx); Kid GT, the racer (a salesman at Best Buy); Solo, more of a generalist (who collects coins from video arcades at night). There seems to be little disagreement among them. About anything. Do they fight about who gets the television?

No. Do they compete with other groups? No. Mostly they just train one another. "Like sparring," Longshot tells me.

The room fills. They haven't gathered like this in a while. "Ever since that MTV show," Suicide Bob says, "people know us as the gamers. They know what we have in here. We let people get a look inside. Big mistake."

"Big mistake," another echoes.

Controllers click and natter like squirrels all around me. Depending on what day it is, depending on whom you ask, there are eight or ten or thirteen members of the Order. Only three live in the apartment, but the others come and go freely. To a man, they are funny and sweet. They explain each game to me slowly, in sort of a loud voice, as if I were a very old man, which I guess I am in this place.

Soon we've been here for four hours. Maybe longer. The shades are drawn. It might be noon, or it might be suppertime. You can never tell. Four of them sit on the couch in semidarkness, eyes turned toward the television, one of them playing a combat video game called Soul Caliber II. The other three watch. My children are seated at their feet. The men—and they are men (twenty-six, thirty-one, twenty-seven, twenty-five years old)—sit in various stages of dress, in poses that reflect a kind of mutual indifference to conversation. One reclines, fusses with his shoes; one flips through a gaming magazine; the other plays. All the while, they do nothing but talk, but not to one another really. It's more like a running commentary.

"I will not be defeated."

"You gotta love Ivy. Just for her outfits."

"I don't see why you don't play it arcade style."

"I will not. I suck. No."

"I mean, come on."

"It's way easier to manipulate that way."

"I can't block! I cannot get off that block."

"You'd think those breasts would get in the way."

"I will not be defeated."

When it gets late enough, when night takes over completely, some of them will rise and head to work. Others, coming off work, will take their place. It's like this all the time, I'm told. They will change the game or the platform, from Xbox to PlayStation 2 to GameCube. The night will roll into day, then back into night again. The gaming will not stop. Four men, then two; six men, then eight, then two again. The simple layout of the apartment, by accident of design, mandates that they face east when they look at the television screen. Away from the door. Away from the road. Away from their work. Away from the city. To the east. Toward the television. Toward the sunrise, such as it is.

Suicide Bob wants to put the helicopter in the garage. The game is Grand Theft Auto: Vice City. It's a trick he taught himself. It took him like thirty minutes the first time, and he couldn't make the turn at first without catching a blade, and then the whole thing would just blow up. Now he can get the helicopter in there sometimes in five minutes, if he pushes evenly and makes the turn into the garage in one swoop.

Then what does he have? Well, the helicopter is in the garage for one thing, which is, well, hilarious. There's nothing you can do with the helicopter in the garage. It's no advantage or anything. It's just something to do. Once it's in the garage, the game puts wheels on it. Also hilarious. Months ago, he taught himself how to push the boat all the way to the garage. Why? His answer—simple, existential, adolescent—befits him: "Because it was a Sunday."

He figures it will take him ten minutes, tops, to get the helicopter in. "It's just a glitch," he says. "I wanted to be the first to discover it."

After that, he wants a Coke.

Suicide Bob has a real name. Everybody knows that. But he picked the nickname long ago and it just took off. Suicide Bob. There's a logic to it, he says. When you play with him, you will die. Hence Suicide. The Bob part is a little trickier. It's plain. Unspectacular. It conveys anonymity, averageness. But there's irony in this. Suicide Bob knows as much. He wants you to concentrate on the Suicide part. There is a kamikaze spirit at work. He's an Eastern warrior. You'd better call him Suicide Bob.

Sometimes while he's playing, Suicide Bob drops into a sequence of martial-arts positions: a kata. He grabs the toe of his sneaker and tugs on his Achilles. He's not deep enough in his squat, and his back is starting to bother him. He should stretch while he games. He reminds himself to remind himself. He is twenty-six years old. He wears jeans and black sneakers and T-shirts, which he mostly scams from different places: Babbage's, the Electronics Boutique, the arcade, gaming conventions. He has a cool one on now. The Green Lantern. Just the logo on a black field. It looks fucking tough. As a gamer, he can't lay claim to much more than that.

He talks as he plays, without looking up: "I'm not really best at any one thing. I learned a long time ago that there's always someone better than you. I'm more of an explorer. Some of these games, they scare the shit out of guys. I'm the one who doesn't blink. I'm the guy who isn't afraid of anything—not zombies, not mutant dogs. Fearless."

In the parking lot outside his bedroom, a car horn sounds. Suicide Bob growls. He does not move his eyes from the screen. "I do not like the day," he says. These grandiose statements act as a kind of self-narration, which suits him, since he claims his life feels for all the world like a comic book. "I like the idea of us as a comic book," he says of the Order of Light, "with each of us having superpowers." He gestures around his room, as if the air in the apartment holds the answers he is looking for. "The problem with superpower is narrowing it down, making it something challenging, finding the right match for your personality." He sits down. Then he stands up again, pulls at his T-shirt. He sniffs.

When you get him outside, Suicide Bob looks light and jumpy. He doesn't much care where he lives. He regards the buildings in his complex with a kind of dull indifference, a reflection of the architecture itself. He knows no one there, just the boys in the Order, and no one else gives him a second look—not the woman who lives in the three-bedroom across the breezeway, not the Mexicans playing stickball in the parking lot, not the three guys who share a two-bedroom across the lot.

He leaves the complex at 9:00 p.m., drives to the FedEx facility on the south side of Memphis, parks his car, takes a shuttle, walks through a tunnel and over a bridge. He drops his stuff, goes to the waiting area, and climbs on a truck with eight or nine other loaders and unloaders. They then drive out to the tarmac and wait for their assigned plane. "I just try to get from point A to point B," Suicide Bob says. "Everyone has a bunch of doors to get through. It's not unlike a game, really."

At 10:00 p.m., the commercial air traffic in Memphis shuts down. It's then that the FedEx planes began to touch down. FedEx controls the skies of Memphis at night. "I've stood there and seen six, eight, ten sets of landing lights," says Suicide Bob. "An hour later, if I remember to look at the sky, they're still coming." He can muster no passion for the scene. He peppers everything he says with a shrug or a smirk.

The planes land continuously for three hours. You might compare them to insects, he says, if you are prone to seeing the world that way, but it's too organized, too fully expected, to be akin to any sort of invasion. It's more like a postmodern assembly line, a nightly production without product. "We really aren't making anything," he says. "Except time." They work with a kind of coldness and familiarity related to watching the clock, because in a matter of hours the planes will be turned around and pushed back out into the world in one enormous rush.

He likes FedEx well enough, because it offers him benefits for what amounts to part-time work. He gets discount shipping, too, and soon the company will be offering a jump seat again on any FedEx plane going anywhere, as it had before September 11. He took advantage only once a year back then, to go to the annual gaming convention. "I've been offered promotions like six times," he says of his four years at FedEx. "I must have some sort of record." He never accepts. "I like my hours. I go home when most people hit that really tough part of a full shift. I want no part of it."

He is living a life that is vaguely sturdy—regular hours, benefits, a car of his own, a closet full of clothes, a full inventory of obscure anime posters, outdated games, even a few action figures still in their original packaging—and yet utterly without weight.

It seems normal to wonder where he came from, but his story is spotty and incomplete. "I'm always in the middle of a phase," he says. He went to college in Virginia. "Nova-coco," he says plaintively, as if that explains all. He's this way with everything—puzzles, games, conversation. You give him a shrug and he gives you the punch line: "Northern Virginia Community College." He lasted six weeks. Then he planned to work in an arcade. "The guy I was counting on sort of flaked on me," he says without elaborating. When his parents moved to Memphis, he drifted along. What drew him to the Order of Light? "I found guys I liked. And you have to have a home. A home base." He lowers his voice, makes it grizzly and harsh, as if he were narrating a commercial for his life: "I'm a soldier. That's my base camp." Even he laughs at the paucity of that comparison.

\ \ \

There is precisely nothing wrong with the Order of Light. It has rules. No drugs. No drinking. No one fights. There is no hazing. There is no gambling. No cursing. No hard feelings. Members don't watch much television, though there are televisions everywhere you look. They aren't fat, but it may be that they rarely eat. Almost everyone goes to church, generally with their parents. Nothing bad. Nothing at all.

They don't love one another, not in any real sense of the world. It's hard to imagine any of them using the word *love*, outside of describing their passion for a game. But there is a pervasive sense of like in this room. These are young men, but, oddly, they don't compete. Instead, they make room for one another. They each have a role, a specialty: one is a hunter and killer, one is a racer, one is a survival gamer, one likes horror, one is a role player. They watch one another play more than they play one another. And when they do play, one of them agrees to be fodder for the other. There are no rivalries, no competition. There's a sort of bloodless respect for the time they each devote to the games. It is a hive, this apartment, each member doing his part, staying out of the way, coming in under the sunrise or at nightfall.

Hours. Days. Years. Youth. Money. The things most people see dwindling in their own lives—these guys appear to have them banked, locked. They have ownership over the time they spend. They have friends. "It's a bond," says Longshot, who is thirty-one and a dangerous-goods agent for FedEx. "You need bonds. We just took advantage of what we were—guys who liked each other, guys who enjoyed the same thing. We just gave it a name." He speaks with the smoke-soft accent of northern Mississippi, earnest beyond belief. He wants you to believe in the Order. It was his doing, gathering the boys together like this, years ago.

They play through everything, every reminder of normalcy and routine—dinner, sleep, sunrise. "For a long time," says Longshot, "we were all into Halo. You could sit right here, and there'd be guys in every room shouting at each other and their teammates. We'd play for eleven hours, then get up and eat. I mean, you worry about your legs. You could say it consumed us."

There isn't much fear here, no sense among the Order that they are wasting time, that something might be slipping away from them. They know the things they will be asked. Yes, they have plans. Yes, they want more. Yes, they have their reasons.

"We do this to stay out of trouble," Longshot says.

"We do it to stay safe," says D.

"The streets are dangerous," says Suicide Bob. "Not a great place to be."

But these are pat answers. Yes, there is danger in Memphis. And decay, too. But it's a good twelve miles from here, over the top of a half dozen shopping malls, several parks, and an interstate.

Press them on their plans for the future and the answers seem so unthreatening and familiar that they might be coming from the mouths of dolls. One is saving money to move to the West Coast. It should be a year. Another is taking flying lessons. It should take four years. Longshot is six hours away from a mathematics degree at the University of Memphis. "It's just a matter of electives for me now. They keep tripping me up." What's the trouble? "I'm a math major. They're making me take classes I don't want." Like what? He adjusts his glasses. "Just classes I don't want." He failed one this semester, he says. What class? "A dumb one," he says. What class? He sighs. "Something called 'Men and Women.'"

I press here and there. The guys know about Iraq but can't tell me much about it. They don't seem to think I'd believe them even if they tried. I wouldn't have, either.

There is a boom box in the corner, but I heard no music in the time I was there, save the fighter themes. Otherwise no stereo. No radio. It is a tangle of nothing, this room.

I have to admit that for a short time on our second day there, I sort of lose sight of my kids. They blend right in. I could have left them there, I think, for days, and these guys—this order, this brotherhood, this family, this army—would have pulled them in. In general, Gus and Walt would have been looked out for, I figure, though they wouldn't have been washed or watched or tended to in any sense. There are no signs of toothbrushes or soap in the bathroom. Nothing is made or managed or much cared for, save the games, which are held with the reverence of communion wafers. My boys would have been safe, however, because I was entirely certain they would not have left that room again if they didn't have to.

I keep telling myself that nine men together are better than nine men on their own. I want to believe that. I know they aren't hurting anyone. And it's impossible not to like the thought of living a life like this, as cozy and snug as a children's book. These guys don't ask much. Their comforts are small, attainable, taxing no one. It's a remarkable kind of freedom really, so vaguely righteous, so oddly libertarian, that it's almost completely American. But I can't for the life of me tell what they want.

I do know what I want. I want to grab them by the shoulders and shake them. Then I want to get my kids out of there.

We left the next day, the boys and I. We managed to say goodbye to some of the Order, but many had slipped away, to work, to sleep, to run errands for their mothers. I shook Suicide Bob's hand at the door. I asked him his real name, since we had been calling him only Bob for months now.

"It's Tim," he said, facing the sunlight from his doorway.

"Tim," I repeated.

"See what I mean?" Suicide Bob said. "Tim. It's a common name. There's a whole world of Tims out there." He waved his hands to the west, out past me. "That's the importance of being Bob. That's when I don't have to be Tim."

We said our goodbyes, and they stood in the doorway waving, polite to the end. They shut the door and locked it behind them.

Gus had held his own against the Order of Light the day before, winning three close games of Halo, losing one. No one in the room seemed to care. Gus appeared deflated as we headed north. I asked him what was up. He was mum.

Walter pulled off his earphones and leaned forward. "I'll tell you what bothers me," he said. "The ambition thing."

I laughed. He sounded like an old man.

He went on. "I mean, they can fly anywhere they want in the whole world, right? Isn't that what they meant by the jump seat, right? And they don't go anywhere. I'd go to Malaysia at least."

Gus snorted. "You're stupid, Walter. It's so dangerous there. Al Qaeda is there. Big time. You should go to Australia instead, dumb ass."

"I'll go where I want to go," said Walter. "I like Malaysia. Or Hawaii."

"Well, you're stupid if you go there. Personally, I'd go to New Zealand."

Walter nodded, "Yeah! Or to France."

They went on like this, arguing the world. I sighed, happy for some combativeness, for a little manufactured conflict. These were my boys. This was our order.

Then Gus looked at me. "I'll tell you one thing I figured out."

"What's that?" I said. We were only minutes outside Memphis.

"I am going to play football this year."

"You don't know how to play football," his little brother said.

"Well, I'm going to. That's all I know. I am going to play football."

"Then we both are," said Walter.

Gus turned to me. "You can teach us the rules, right? I mean, you can teach us, can't you?"

MY LIFE, MY LOSS

by Jake LaMotta as told to Cal Fussman

Me bein' married six times, I'm gonna have to give you a joke with that. You know what it means to come home to a beautiful, lovely, gorgeous lady who gives you a lot of love, affection, and tenderness? It means you're in the wrong goddamn apartment.

It helps to have a sense of humor. Better to have one than not have one. Better to be up instead of down, right? After everything that happened, I'm telling you . . . I couldn't sleep for six months. I went from one extreme to another. All my life I made a living out of hurting people. Now I make people laugh. Helps get me through the day.

So you wanna know about my father. One day when I was a kid, I came home crying. Some older kid took my sandwich and banged me around some. My father slapped me, gave me an ice pick, and said, "Here, hit him back with this! Don't never run away from nobody. If you ever come home crying again, I'll beat the crap out of ya. Ya understand?"

A few days later, three kids ganged up on me and were giving it to me pretty good when I remembered what my father told me. I caught one of them with the ice pick across the cheek, ripped his skin, and when the other kids saw blood, you should have heard their screams as they ran away. I guess you could say my father and growin' up in the Bronx made me a fighter.

People ask me how to take a punch. I tell 'em it's like catching a hardball in a baseball glove. When the ball is just about to hit your hand, you move the glove back and take 80 percent of the power away as you catch it. Same thing in a fight. The trick is to see the punch comin', then move with it. If I took all those punches solid, believe me, I wouldn't be speaking to you coherently at this moment.

That reminds me of the one about Rocky Graziano. When Rocky fought Tony Zale, Tony had him on the canvas. His manager kept yelling to Rocky, "Stay down till eight! Stay down till eight!" And Rocky says, "Uhhh, what time is it now?"

You like that one?

The jokes, they help keep my mind off everything that happened with my sons. I try to knock it away, not to think about it. But sometimes I get caught off guard. Like getting hit before you can see the punches comin'. Sometimes I'm telling my jokes and I can hear myself stuttering. All of a sudden I can't talk right. At night, I go home and I can't sleep. Both of my sons in seven months. Nobody lives forever, I know. But why? *Why?*

In a way, I blame myself for Jack. He was always complaining about pains in his stomach. He should have taken care of it. We went to Paris one time, and we had to stop the car, he had such excruciating pain. But he didn't believe in doctors, like I don't believe in doctors. I told him, "This is something important. It's no black eye. When nature's trying to warn you, you have to listen." As the months passed, he started to change, to get yellow. I told him, "Go to the doctor!" But it was too late. Cancer. He never should have died.

And Joe—that was, that was, that was . . . I blame myself for it. If I never went to Switzerland, he never would have gone, either. We came home. Then he decided to go back there for business. My lawyer was supposed to be on the same flight, Swissair 111, but at the last minute my lawyer didn't go. Then the plane went down, and my lawyer called me and told me that Joe was dead.

After the crash, I got calls from all over. Mayor Giuliani. The pope of New York wanted to meet me—what's his name, O'Connor? They did a service at St. Patrick's Cathedral. People would stop me in the street—men, women, kissing me, telling me how sorry they feel. I musta got hundreds and hundreds of letters. So much was happening that it didn't seem to hit me right away. I thought I took it OK. I don't know. Maybe I was in shock. Aw, I'm tellin' ya, it's better not to think about it.

You see that guy over there? The boss. He must've heard my jokes half a dozen times, but he always laughs. I got the type of jokes you could tell over and over and people keep laughin'. You wanna hear some more? The greatest pleasure I get now is makin' people laugh.

But if I start stuttering when I tell 'em, you know why.

A FEW WORDS FROM
SONS

ME AND SANDY THE BULL

by Scott Raab

I find my father everywhere—in the mirror, of course, in the cupid's bow of my four-year-old son's lips, in the tugging of my heart toward rage even as my hair goes white, and in the hate and hurt whetted in my family's soul. I find my father because I want to find him, because I grew up without him, starving for him, because I'm still greedy to redeem our love.

Mainly, though, I find him because Sandy Raab is hard to miss. See that three-hundred-pound, seventy-six-year-old guy with the Gabby Hayes beard, the stogie stuck in his pie hole, the pecker-tracked sweatpants, and the food-crusted turquoise T-shirt? That'd be him. That's my old man.

I'm in Laughlin, Nevada, back in 1997. I'm working on a story—nasty story, nasty town—but I have a couple of days to kill, so I call L.A. And invite Sandy to come gamble and pillage the buffets with me.

"How far is it from Los Angeles?"

Five hours.

"You need cigars?"

No.

"How far is it from Los Angeles?"

I just told you.

"Don't be a wiseass. You said five hours. How many miles?"

Three hundred.

"You need cigars?"

Dad, I don't smoke cigars.

"Putz. You don't know what you're missing. See you in a couple hours."

The first thing we do is slay a herd of three-buck prime rib. Then Sandy lays his hands on quarter slots until he finds an adjacent pair that feel warm and giving. Two hours later, up a combined $190, we go strolling behind the row of casinos along the Colorado River.

Frankie Valli is yowling behind a fence. We can't see him, but we sure can hear him. Dead fish on the river's bottom can hear him. Coyotes foraging the bluffs at the edge of the desert sky can hear him. It is truly not a good thing to hear, but here's a bench—so here we sit.

Sandy torches a Macanudo. Soon, a pear-shaped security guard appears. "I'm sorry, folks," he says, "but you're going to have to keep moving."

"*What?*" My father has been honing this one-word, all-purpose snarl for years. It is loud and querulous, timed—like a snapping left jab—to land before his opponent has finished a sentence.

"I'm sorry, sir. You can't sit here." Polite, deferential. He sees my father's arms, like stanchions; sees the beard of white stubble; sees the cast of his eyes, the red glare that warns: I am insane.

"*I'm smokin' a cigar.*"

"Yessir, but you can't smoke it here. Not during the concert."

Dad, let's go.

"*I'm smokin' a cigar. I'm not listening to that little greaseball.*"

Let's go, Dad.

Back to the slots. We're surrounded by the living dead; even the cocktail waitresses are shriveled, their long wrinkles caked with powder, thighs bulging through their fishnets like forcemeat. My father looks glum. The belly of his T-shirt is ash streaked and stained with the dried blood of his dinner.

Ready to cash in, Dad?

"*What?* You're tired?"

I've got an early interview with a cop.

He shrugs, frowning, scanning the room, the stump of his last cigar cold between clenched teeth.

"If you wanted a whore in this place," says my father, "you'd have to wheel her up."

My father is looking for his father. I'm helping. His way of looking is to ask me to look; my way of looking is to dick around for an hour on the computer, Googling a name my father can't spell, the name of a man I never met. Then I find something better to do, something more productive, like waiting for the mail.

His dad died in or about 1951, in or around New York City, and was buried in a potter's field—the old term for a paupers' boneyard. His first name in Yiddish was Velvel; he went by Willie in America. My father says he came from Poland via South America, with a lengthy, unpronounceable last name—devoid of any vowels except for y—that later became Piltz.

Willie used other last names. One, according to an undated, photocopied clipping from an old Cleveland newspaper, was Pelz. My father gave me the clip years ago. "William" Pelz had been shot in the chest and groin by a jealous man. Pelz's wife of four weeks—formerly the jealous man's lover—also had been shot, in the head. The shooter owned a steak house; the newlyweds were working in the restaurant kitchen when he shot them.

The jealous man was just out of prison, a bootlegger and arsonist. Pelz's new wife, Gertrude—not my dad's mom, although, as far as he knows, his parents never were divorced—also had done time in prison for bootlegging. As for Willie, the clipping says that he was fifty-seven when he was shot and that his criminal record dated back to 1915—twelve years before my father was born.

Willie was no kind of father. He was nothing but a small-time Cleveland hood—a shakedown artist, a bomb roller during the dry cleaners' war, a rumrunner, a playboy, a bigamist. The family—Sandy was the youngest of five children—ran from tenement to tenement in the tough-Jew Kinsman ghetto when they couldn't make rent. In 1937, when my dad was ten, Willie went to jail, to Lewisburg Federal Penitentiary—this, too, is in the clip—for "conspiracy to violate liquor laws."

Stone poor, hopeless, my dad's mother downsized, which is how my father became Sanford Raab. He went to live with his uncle, his mother's brother Julius Raab, who legally adopted him. This could've been a decent break for Sandy—Julius lived up in Cleveland Heights and was a medical doctor—but for two things: one, my father believed that his mother had sold him to Doc Raab, which wounded him terribly; and two, Julius was no picnic, despite his income and status. Rabinowitz was his surname when he got off the boat, and he was a prick.

Julius, too, was destined for Lewisburg—he had built a thriving abortion practice, and, ratted out by a competitor, pleaded guilty to tax evasion. By that time, my dad had enlisted in the Navy, fresh out of high school. He was going to classes at Kent State on the GI Bill when one of his sisters phoned from New York to say that Velvel was on his deathbed. She asked Sandy to come and say goodbye to his dad. He didn't.

My father wants to visit his old man now; he just can't find the grave.

\ \ \

A Depression ghetto child, Sandy had two basic choices: lay down and die, or be a tough guy. And though it's nice to think that you'll adapt when you get to a certain age or a different stage in your life—a happier place, maybe, with better choices and more resources—that hasn't happened with my father.

Not long ago, something his boss had said about him a few days earlier got back to him and pissed him off. So Sandy Raab—half deaf, diapered and diabetic, sleep-apncic and bipolar, incontinent and impotent after a bout with prostate cancer, with no pension, no credit, and nothing in the bank—rang his boss on the cell phone his boss pays for and asked if his boss had made the remark.

Yup.

"*Fuck* you, then," my father said. "I quit."

My father told me this story on the phone.

"You'd have done the same thing," he added.

Maybe not, I said.

"Well, he called me back the next day to apologize. So I'm still working for the sonuvabitch."

My first reaction was relief. In the last two years, my father has hit up two of my brothers for money—he always needs pocket money for books, cigars, and Viagra. Both brothers said no; one even had the gall to ask why he needed the cash, which hurt Sandy's feelings. I knew he was hurt because after he told me about the turndown, he added, "Fuck him."

"You woulda loaned me the money," he said.

Not without a promissory note and a repayment schedule.

"*Fuhhhhck* you," my father said.

The man is cranky, yes—so am I. But that doesn't make us any less sensitive or sincere. One way or another, we settle all accounts. When my father comes to visit us in New Jersey, I pay his way and he repays me, a chunk at a time. The checks come randomly—no note, nothing else in the envelope. On the last one he sent, he'd written "0 balance" on the memo line.

Zero balance: He had that right. For the plane fare. I'm still out for the hand-cut lox, the pastrami and corned beef, the rib roast, the pastry, the tube of denture-adhesive cream, the laxative, and the downstairs toilet he destroyed. He's a hard-nosed motherfucker, my old man. And so am I.

He never finished his degree from Kent State. In 1950, he married my mother, Lucille, and went to work selling clothes, first as a retailer—his dress shop on Superior Avenue was named Sandy-Lu's—and then, when the shop went belly-up in the early fifties, he sold wholesale on the road, ladies' foundational garments, bras and girdles, to shops in central and southern Ohio and northern Kentucky.

I arrived in 1952, firstborn of my parents' three sons, the nine-pound-five-ounce heir, King Sanford's brooding little prince. I missed him when he traveled, missed him bad. I'd watch the Friday-night fights on TV with him; he was a serious fight fan. He'd done some boxing in the Navy, when he was skinny, and he doted on the middleweights. Sugar Ray Robinson was his paragon, but it was a fine era for that weight class, and I remember sitting at my dad's feet as the Fullmer brothers, Gene and Don, and Carmen Basilio banged away, bleeding on the little screen.

My brother Dave came along in 1955—don't ask me why; the last thing I wanted was competition—and my dad got off the road and took a job in someone else's clothing store. After he quit that, he managed a carpet-and-tile barn. He hated retail—his bosses, his customers, the dead hours and dead air, the crap pay. He hated himself, too, and toughed out long spells of melancholy.

He wanted me tough. I understood that from the get go, from watching him. He pumped a pair of iron dumbbells until his biceps became rock. He wasn't much bigger than your average Joe—a shade under six feet, 190 pounds or so—but his shoulders and chest were tight and thick; his forearms, too. Sandy Raab was a bull. I worshiped him, the muscle and the smell of him—Old Spice and smoke and sweat. My dad smelled like man. Not *a* man: Man.

I wanted to be tough, but I was too young to understand what it meant or what it cost: the isolation from feeling, the pure hurt of it. One day, I went at it tooth and nail with the bully of the block while my dad sat in his chair on the concrete slab we called a porch and read his paper. I was five or six—the same age as the bully, and no smaller—and I took a whupping. I was furious with my father for not budging.

"You have to fight your own battles," he said. "Anyway, you held your own."

Not long after, I whined about some other kid picking on me.

"Hit him back," he said.

But he's bigger than me.

"Then pick up a rock and hit him with that," he told me.

Funny thing is, my dad was no primitive. He had a .38 and a lot of hard-guy friends, but he also kept a stash of books from his brief college days—a Freud biography, some Hemingway and Henry Miller, and a one-volume collection of Shakespeare. He was tough and he was bookish, but in reality he was just a guy in a carpet-and-tile store, in his thirties now, feeling the walls of his life closing in a little more every day.

Meanwhile, Julius Raab had done his time, lost his medical license, and gone west to Los Angeles. He had money and real estate connections, and he offered Sandy a house in the San Fernando Valley, which was ranch- and farmland in 1960. Millions of people were headed there—walls were closing in on a lot of guys my dad's age—and my father persuaded my mother to make the move. She had just given birth to my brother Bob a few weeks before we packed up and left Cleveland.

My dad and I left first, by car. My mom and brothers flew out a couple of weeks later. I was eight, my father was thirty-three, and that trip with him was paradise. Whatever Sandy was searching for then, I was by his side.

We took Route 66—the Mother Road—and read aloud the signpost poetry of Burma Shave. We stopped to see caverns and Indians, taverns and cafés, purple mountains, fruited plains, the Mojave Desert, and motels with swimming pools. One night, as we pulled out of Albuquerque just before sunrise, the moon hung in the sky so big and bone white that he stopped to get out and look up at it. It filled the sky and I fell down. I fell down on my back right there beside the road, trembling with awe.

Beyond any and all of this, there was my dad. I was his beloved son, and he—he was all mine. We were together. We were on the road. He loved me: it was knitted in my soul. And I loved my old man, with a love more primal and helpless, more powerful and fierce, than I'd know again for nearly forty years—until the afternoon I kissed my newborn boy, my own sweet son, Judah Raab.

When I'm working in L.A.—two or three times a year—I'll spend as much time as I can with Sandy, which has come to mean only as much time as I can stand. If we're on our way to eat, or eating, or driving home from a meal—fine. Everything else is a crapshoot. We argue, then he falls asleep.

A while back, before his prostate cancer, I was staying at a swank hotel on Sunset, waiting three days for my two hours with Nicolas Cage. My father came down to wait with me one day. We ate a big room-service breakfast, then an enormous room-service lunch. From the trays and platters dead on the bed, you'd have thought we'd been holed up for weeks.

I needed the bathroom for a number two. While I was in there, Sandy had to go number one. *Had* to go, bad. But he didn't knock on the john door or say boo—he just took himself a nice, long pee in the wastebasket by my desk. And laughed about it, too.

He's not senile yet, my old man: he just doesn't give a damn. He'll tell a waitress that her service sucked. He'll flip the bird if you cut him off, and he has been known, even in his Medicare years, to pull over if you'd like a piece of him. His inner gangster, the shade of Willie, never went away. Sometimes now I'll go out there and never let him know I'm in town. When I'm on the road working that cruel celebrity beat, I need to be clear and sharp, ready to go at a moment's . . . Ahhhh, *fuck* me. Truth is, I can't handle L.A., the capital of empty-head, self-serve bullshit, and I can't handle my father, either. I'm not proud of not calling him, nor am I ashamed. Nobody taught him how to be a father or a son. And as for what he taught me—well, that's for Judah to judge when his own search unfolds.

I liked L.A. Fine as a kid, but it didn't last long. Less than two years after we moved out there, I came home from school one day and my mother told me we were going back to Cleveland. Without Dad.

This was 1962, when divorce was rare, and it was not amicable. There was a villain named Sandy, a victim named Lucille, and three innocent boys. We hadn't heard them fighting. Nobody suggested counseling. It was over just like that. Done. I was ten.

I don't remember saying goodbye to my father. I don't remember anyone explaining one damn thing to me. What I do recall is my mother saying we couldn't take our dog back to Cleveland with us because the climate change would kill him. I was smart enough to realize that she was lying, that the Cleveland weather wasn't going to kill the dog.

I don't know what happened to the dog, but for me—and for my father and me—life ran downhill fast. Lucille took us back to Cleveland and her folks took us in. I didn't merely miss my dad; I ached for him. There was no money for long-distance calls, and his letters were few and far between. I'd see him for a week or so in the summer if he came to Cleveland, or a couple of weeks if Dave and I were sent out to L.A., but it wasn't every year and it wasn't nearly enough.

I did hear a lot about him. Not by eavesdropping—direct from my mother. Sandy slept around; he made lousy money and threw away the little he made buying things for himself—a hi-fi, beer, steaks; he was a bastard and I was just like him. I heard it all.

To say that my mother, too, was shocked and hurting and afraid—stigmatized as a divorcée, penniless and unprepared for any type of job, saddled with three sons and forced back under her parents' roof—is not to deny that this was poor parenting. It was ugly stuff, cruel, fanged with a full measure of female venom. The worst was when she told me that my father didn't really love me.

Didn't love me? I wasn't buying that, but, my God, it hurt to hear it—and it didn't endear my mother to me. Don't get me wrong: I'm grateful to Lucille for not selling me. But I always felt like if she'd had a decent offer, she wouldn't have turned it down.

I got bigger and stronger, and I got tough. My brothers paid the physical price for that; I paid the rest. I stopped giving a shit about school or much of anything. I had sports, boxing in particular; rock 'n' roll; and books—as long as they weren't any of the books I was supposed to read. Then I started writing. Later, drugs. I'd dabble in crime, guns, and women, but only with drugs and writing did I ever feel truly tough enough to be in charge.

As for Sandy, he was back in California. It didn't take him long to remarry and to sire another son, my brother Michael.

Sandy flew into Newark in December 1999 to see Judah for the first time. I met him at the airport, alone. I was feeling pretty proud—a forty-seven-year-old man with an infant son tends to feel that way.

Newark's not an easy airport. By the time we got his bags and started circling for the Garden State Parkway ramp, he was telling me how proud he was of me, and of my work, of how I stuck with writing, of how I never gave it up even though I got no help from anyone.

It's tricky, getting on the parkway. Miss the first ramp, you're on your way to New York City; miss the second, you're on Interstate 78. Luckily, I can drive and seethe at the same time. My stomach began churning: I knew what was coming, because I'd heard numerous versions of the same crap from him. Don't get me wrong: I want my dad to be proud of me. But we've both read better writers, and we both know the road to Stockholm isn't paved with magazine profiles.

"I'm disappointed, though," my father said, "that you haven't written a book."

If *you're* disappointed, how the fuck do you think I feel?

"*Hmp,*" my father said.

I don't want to hear any of that shit. We're not even out of the fucking airport loop yet.

"I'm hungry," my father said.

Me, too.

By the time I started college, my dad and I were hardly in touch.

Whatever I was searching for, I had no idea how to begin. Women scared me. School bored me. But the drugs were cheap and excellent, and the dorm vending machines were full of loose change if you hit them hard enough with a crowbar.

Past forty now, Sandy was going to college, too. He was working at RCA, and he'd ridden an employee tuition-assistance program to a bachelor's degree—and started night law school while working full-time.

I went out to L.A. To see him in the summer of '71, between my freshman and sophomore years. Whatever shell of tough I'd made for myself was cracking. I had moved from wine and weed to Jim Beam and 'ludes, and from vending machines to burglary; my best friend broke open my skull during a fight, then drove me to the ER and waited while I got stitched up; my GPA was headed south of 1.0. I needed a firmer hand than my own.

My father knew nothing about any of this, of course. He hooked me up with the worst job I've ever had, in a plating room, 6:00 a.m. To 4:00 p.m. Six days a week for two bucks an hour. There were bikers, ex-cons, wetbacks, and me. I did amphetamines every day, got my first two tattoos on the Pike in Long Beach, and lost seventy pounds I needed to lose. My dad and I hardly ever saw each other; when we did, my head was buzzing so loud I couldn't hear a word he said.

I dropped out of college that fall, hitched from Cleveland back to L.A., and moved in with my dad. He was forty-five and becoming a lawyer was life and death to him. I was nineteen and out of control. I needed my old man, and he took me in, no questions asked. But even if he'd known how, he couldn't father me through the ten years we'd already lived apart. The lessons he'd taken from Willie and Julius—how to be tough, followed by how to disappear—would have to do.

I lasted six months under his roof. He was pissed when I left, and I didn't blame him a bit. He was humping for the bar exam; I was dropping acid on the beach and staying gone three days at a stretch without calling. It was past time for me to go, but he wasn't about to make it easy on me. He bought my car for what I'd paid for it—$150—and I wound up calling my mother for the rest of the cash for a plane ticket back to Cleveland.

I remember saying goodbye to my father then. "Go," he sneered. "Run back to your mommy."

Sandy passed the bar. I didn't stay two weeks with my mommy: I got a job selling shoes.

My son's afraid of dragons, dinosaurs, and skeletons.

"Will you protect me?"

I will protect you. That is part of my job, to protect you. No dragons. No dinosaurs. No skeletons. If we see one, I will pinch its head like a grape.

"Thanks."

You're welcome.

I can handle the dragons, dinosaurs, and skeletons, and I've got my pistol-grip Mossberg 12-gauge to deal with the other stuff. Still, I find myself unable to sleep, worried sick, full of fear. I'm fifty and a father now, and given the lessons of fatherhood I learned from Sandy—how to be tough, followed by how to disappear—who'll protect Judah from me?

My old man resigned from RCA, went into practice with a night-school pal, and snapped like a twig. What should have been a glorious march—from poor boy to attorney-at-law—collapsed into Sandy sitting in a rented office on Ventura Boulevard, unable to answer the ringing phone. It was Sandy's first round with full-blown organic depression—and depression knocked his hard ass down and out.

If I knew about his breakdown then, I don't remember; I was busy keeping numb. Man, oh man, I was tough. I rented a forty-dollar-a-month room in a creaky old house and carried a .22 when I stepped out. I think I saw my dad once in L.A. During the rest of the seventies—I've got a photo of myself and Michael in L.A., dated 1975—and I guess he came to Cleveland once. I was loaded all day every day for a lot of years.

I moved to Texas in '78, washed out as a drug dealer there, and caught a train back to Cleveland in '80, a step ahead of guys much tougher than me and my old man combined. I returned to college—Cleveland State University, the Harvard of Euclid Avenue—and when I got married for the first time in 1982, I called my dad to invite him.

We hadn't spoken in years, but he came to the wedding. It was good to see him. He was a businessman, not a lawyer, working for an electronics company. It was a short visit, and it was low-key. I was very glad he'd come, and so was he.

Next time I saw him wasn't good. I was in Iowa, in grad school; he came to visit for four days in 1985. He'd been in Singapore for a year, negotiating contracts, overseeing production, living large—too large. Sandy was the size of Colonel Kurtz, and his head was exploding. After driving him from the Cedar Rapids airport to the Iowa City Holiday Inn—the ritziest lodging in town, fifty-five dollars per night—I carried his bags up for him and sat on the bed as he went to the bathroom. He didn't bother closing the door, and while my father moved his bowels, he told me about a woman he was deeply, madly in love with.

When he emerged from the toilet, he said that if a word of this ever got back to my stepmother, he would kill me.

What are you gonna do—shoot me?

"Probably," he said. "I will hunt you down, and I will kill you."

He was serious. Me, I was stunned. I went home, got my wife, and drove back to meet him for dinner. We found him at the hotel bar, buying drinks for two women he'd already invited to join us for the evening. In four days at the Holiday Inn in Iowa City, he ran up a bill of eight hundred dollars. He talked incessantly about his Singapore adventures and how the natives there paid homage to him. He was going back, he said, maybe never to return.

I don't remember what my wife said, but his reply was "Fuck you."

Hey—don't talk that way to my wife.

"Fuck you, too," my father said.

The fallout from that visit lasted for years. I sent him an angry letter; what I heard back, from my stepmother months later, was that my father had been diagnosed as manic-depressive and was doing well on medication—and, oh, by the way, the doctors tell us that this thing runs in families, so you need to be aware of that.

I wrote him off. We'd talk on the phone once or twice a year; he sounded comatose. He came back for a few days four years later, sleepy, stripped of energy, a tranquilized bear mumbling vague apologies for his conduct in '85 but recalling none of it. His apologies meant nothing to me, anyway. I didn't know what to make of this drugged, old piece-of-shit father of mine. Maybe I was crazy, maybe not, but at least I was independent: I needed nobody else to tell me what drugs to take.

On his last day in Iowa, I squeezed his groggy carcass into my Ford Festiva and drove to Dyersville, where they'd made *Field of Dreams* the year before. Snow flew, but the baseball diamond was still cut and cleared, and we got in ten minutes of playing catch. Shoeless Joe never emerged from the withered cornstalks. No Costner, no Velvel— just Sandy and me in the blowing snow. It wasn't a movie: it was life.

Everybody fades a little more each day, then disappears for good.

I broke in 1993. I wrecked my marriage beyond fixing and almost did the same with work. Part of it, no doubt, was biochemical, some was circumstance, and a lot of it was the twenty-plus years of drug studies I'd been conducting on myself. You could go nuts parceling out and weighing all the factors, and there was no need for that—I already was full-blown crazy.

I still have a copy of the letter I wrote my dad early in '93. "Dear Sanford Raab," it began, and it was ice all the way, full of formal, impersonal contempt. I closed with, "If you have something more to say, you really ought to try putting some of your thoughts into words on paper. Show me some guts."

I was desperate, falling fast, but still a long way from hitting bottom, and scared to fucking death. I needed my daddy bad—and if you're searching for Sandy Raab, the best way to find him is by challenging his guts. He came through the only way he knows how: I got back a howl scrawled on yellow legal paper.

"Let me tell you about guts . . ." it began, and went on for the full page. "You don't have the balls to face me," he wrote. I was "too much of a coward." "Keep on hiding, sonny boy," he wrote, and he included this invite: "If you are ever in Los Angeles, come see me and an old man will teach you what guts are."

So I called him up and told him I'd be glad to break his jaw, wherever, whenever. I meant it, but I also was crying pretty hard when I said it, and we stayed on the phone for a good, long time. We ended up making plans to meet in Las Vegas a few weeks later to watch Michael Carbajal and Humberto "Chiquita" Gonzalez duke it out for the light-flyweight championship.

It was a great fight, and it was a fresh start for me and my old man.

There was nothing storybook about it—I was too busy destroying the rest of my life to focus too much attention on my father—but in the next letter I got from him, after Vegas, he wrote, "I have never felt so close to another human being in my life." He signed it, "Everlasting love, Dad."

I didn't read that letter from him for a long time, because I knew that it would touch me where I could no longer stand to be touched. I was plenty tough enough to shut the door on love, but I wasn't tough enough yet to put aside the hurt and anger and drugs, open it back up, and walk through like a full-grown man instead of a helpless boy. My father taught me by precept and example that pain and rage, properly distilled, can carry a man a long way in this world, but he couldn't teach me how to love. I'm learning that now from my son. Judah gives me lessons every day.

Things got much worse before getting better. That's the way addiction goes. If you're lucky, you don't kill anybody else and you don't French-kiss your Mossberg. If you're lucky, you find your old man when you need him bad. If you're really lucky, you have a son someday. And if you're both lucky, he knows how and where to find you.

If you're smart, you know the balance between a father and his son is never zero. I owe the hard-nosed motherfucker, and always will. I am the fruit of his loins—same flesh, same blood. I still go looking for the old man. Lucky for Sandy and me, I know just where to find him. I bust his ancient, shrunken balls—and he busts mine. Sure it hurts. Where we came from, that's love.

Happy Father's Day, tough guy.

THE MAN WHO MISTOOK HIS HAT FOR A MEAL

by David Sedaris

We're in Paris, eating dinner in a nice restaurant, and my father is telling a story. "So," he says, "I found this brown something-or-other in my suitcase, and I started chewing on it, thinking that maybe it was part of a cookie."

"Had you packed any cookies?" my friend Maja asks.

My father considers this an irrelevant question and brushes it off, saying, "Not that I know of, but that's not the point."

"So you found this thing in your suitcase, and your first instinct was to put it in your mouth?"

"Well, yes," he says. "Sure I did. But the thing is . . ."

He continues his story, but aside from my sisters and me, his audience is snagged on what would strike any sane adult as a considerable stumbling block. Why would a full-grown man place a foreign object into his mouth, especially if it was brown and discovered in a rarely used suitcase? It is a reasonable question, partially answered when the coffee arrives and my father slips a fistful of sugar into the pocket of his sport coat. Had my friends seen the blackened banana lying on my bed, they might have understood my father's story and enjoyed it on its own merit. As it stood, however, an explanation was in order.

For as long as I can remember, my father has saved. He saves money, he saves disfigured sticks that resemble disfigured celebrities, and, most of all, he saves food. Cherry tomatoes, sausage biscuits, the olives plucked from other people's martinis: he hides these things in strange places until they are rotten. And then he eats them.

I used to think of this as standard Greek behavior until I realized that ours was the only car in the church parking lot consistently swarmed by bees. My father hid peaches in the trunk of his car. He hid pastries in the toolshed and the laundry room and then wondered where all the ants were coming from. Open the cabinet in the master bathroom and, to this day, you will find expired six-packs of Sego, a chalky dietary milk shake popular in the late sixties. Crowded beside liquefied nectarines and rock-hard kaiser rolls, the cans relax, dented and lint covered, against the nastiest shaving kit you have ever seen in your life.

There are those who attribute my father's hoarding to being raised during the Depression, but my mother was not one of them.

"Bullshit," she used to say. "I had it much worse than him, but you don't see me hiding figs."

The reference to figs was telling. My father hid them until they assumed the consistency of tar, but why did he bother? No one else in the family would have gone anywhere near a fig, regardless of its age. There were never any potato chips tucked into his food vaults, no chocolate bars or marshmallow figurines. The question, asked continually throughout our childhood, was, Who is he hiding these things from? Aside from the usual insects and the well-publicized starving people in India, we failed to see any potential takers. You wouldn't catch our neighbors scraping mold off their strawberries, but to our father, there was nothing so rotten that it couldn't be eaten. It was people who were spoiled, not food.

"It's fine," he'd say, watching as a swarm of flies deposited its hatchlings into the decaying flesh of a pineapple. "There's nothing wrong with that. I'd eat it!" And he would, if the price was right. And the price was always right.

Because she fell for words like *fresh-picked* and *vine-ripened,* our mother was defined as a spendthrift. You couldn't trust a patsy like that, especially in the marketplace, and so, armed with a thick stack of coupons, our father did all the shopping himself. Accompanying him to the grocery store, my sisters and I were encouraged to think of the produce aisle as an all-you-can-eat buffet. Tart apples, cherries, grapes, and unblemished tangerines: he was of the opinion that because they weren't wrapped, these things were free for the taking. The store managers thought differently, and it was always just a matter of time before someone was sent to stop him. The head of the produce department would arrive, and my father, his mouth full of food, would demand to be taken into the back room, a virtual morgue where unwanted food rested between death and burial.

Due to the stench and what our mother referred to as "one small scrap of dignity," my sisters and I never entered the back room. It seemed best to distance ourselves, and so we would pretend to be other people's children until our father returned bearing defeated fruits and vegetables that bore no resemblance to those he had earlier enjoyed with such abandon. The message was that if something is free, you should take only the best. If, on the other hand, you're forced to pay, it's best to lower the bar and not be so choosy.

"Quit your bellyaching," he'd say, tossing a family pack of questionable pork chops into the cart. "Meat is supposed to be gray. They doctor up the color for the ads and so forth, but there's nothing wrong with these. You'll see."

I've never known our father to buy anything not marked reduced for quick sale. Without that orange tag, an item was virtually invisible to him. The problem was that he never associated "quick sale" with "immediate consumption." Upon returning from the store, he would put the meat into the freezer, hide his favorite fruits in the bathroom cabinet, and stuff everything else into the crisper. It was, of course, too late for crisp, but he took the refrigerator drawer at its word, insisting it was capable of reviving the dead and returning them, hale and vibrant, to the prime of their lives. Subjected to a few days in his beloved crisper, a carrot would become as pale and soft as a flaccid penis.

"Hey," he'd say. "Somebody ought to eat this before it goes bad."

He'd take a bite, and the rest of us would wince at the unnatural silence. Too weak to resist, the carrot quietly surrendered to the force of his jaws. An overcooked hot dog would have made more noise. Wiping the juice from his lips, he would insist that this was the best carrot he'd ever eaten. "You guys don't know what you're missing."

Oh, I think we had a pretty good idea.

Even at our most selfish, we could understand why someone might be frugal with six children to support. We hoped our father might ease up and learn to treat himself once we all left home, but, if anything, he's only gotten worse. Nothing will convince him that his fortunes might not suddenly reverse, reducing him to a diet of fingernail clippings and soups made from fallen leaves and seasoned with flashlight batteries. The market will collapse or the crops will fail. Invading armies will go door-to-door, taking even our condiments, yet my father will tough it out. Retired now and living alone, he continues to eat like a scavenging bird.

We used to return home for Christmas every year, my brother, sisters, and I making it a point to call ahead, offering to bring whatever was needed for the traditional holiday meal.

"No, I already got the lamb," our father would say. "Grape leaves, phyllo dough, potatoes—I got everything on the list."

"Yes, but *when* did you get these things?"

An honest man except when it comes to food, our father would lie, claiming to have just returned from the pricey new Fresh Market.

"Did you get the beans?" we'd ask.

"Well, sure I did."

"Let me hear you snap one."

Come Christmas day, we would fly home to find a leg of lamb thawing beneath six inches of frost, the purchase date revealing that it had been bought midway through the Carter administration. Age had already mashed the potatoes, the grape leaves bore fur, and it was clear that, when spoken to earlier over the phone, our father had snapped his fingers in imitation of a healthy green bean.

"Why the long faces?" he'd ask. "It's Christmas day. Cheer up, for Christ's sake."

Tired of rancid oleo and "perfectly good" milk resembling bluecheese dressing, my family began taking turns hosting Christmas dinner. This past year, it was my turn, and those who could afford it agreed to join me in Paris. I met my father's plane at Charles de Gaulle, and as we were walking toward the taxi stand, a bag of peanuts fell from the pouch of his suitcase. These were not peanuts handed out on his recent flight but something acquired years earlier, back when all planes had propellers and pilots wore leather helmets and long, flowing scarves.

I picked up the bag and felt its contents crumble and turn to dust. "Give me those, will you?" My father tucked the peanuts into his breast pocket, saving them for later.

Back at the apartment, he unpacked. I thought the cat had defecated on my bed until I realized that the object on my pillow was not a turd but a shriveled black banana he had brought all the way to Paris from its hiding place beneath the bathroom sink.

"Here," my father said. "I'll give you half of it."

He'd brought a pear as well and had wrapped it in a plastic bag so that its pus wouldn't stain the clothing he had packed the day before but bought long before he was married. As with his food, my father is faithful to his wardrobe. Operating on the assumption that, sooner or later, even the toga will make a comeback, he holds on to his clothing and continues to wear things long after they've begun to disintegrate.

Included in his suitcase was a battered suede cap bought in Kansas City shortly after the war. This was the cap that would figure into his story later that night, when we joined my sisters and a few friends at a nice Paris restaurant.

"So," he says, "I found this brown-colored something-or-other in my suitcase, and I must have chewed on the thing for a good five minutes, until I realized I was eating the brim of my cap. Can you beat that? A piece of it must have broken off during the flight—but hell, how was I supposed to know what it was?"

My friend Maja finds this amusing. "So you literally ate your hat?"

"Well, yes," my father says. "But not the whole thing. I stopped after the first bite."

An outsider might think he stopped for practical reasons, but my sisters and I know better. Because it didn't kill him, the cap was proved edible and would now be savored and appreciated in a different way. No longer considered an article of clothing, it would return to its native land, where it would move from the closet to the bathroom cabinet, joining the ranks of the spoiled to wait for the coming famine.

MY FATHER THE SPY

by John H. Richardson

Mom calls. Dad is in the hospital, on oxygen. It's his heart. I fly down. They live in Mexico in a big adobe house with cool tile floors and high ceilings. Servants move quietly through the rooms. Mom greets me at the door, telling me through tears that she found him last night flopped across the bed with his legs hanging off the edge. He couldn't lift his feet onto the bed, so he just lay there like flotsam for an hour before he started calling for help. When she finally woke up, he apologized for bothering her. Then I laugh, and she smiles through her tears, because it's just so Dad. He's always so polite, so maddeningly self-denying. Sometimes my mom cries out: "Don't ask me what I want! Just tell me what you want!"

I go into his room, and his face is puffy and red, and he looks so very weak. With his dentures out and his head back, he looks like a cartoon of an old codger, lips sucked back over his gums and grizzled chin jutting out. One yellowed tooth stands out in the black hole of his mouth. He's like an apple that's been sitting on a shelf for months, all dried out and sucked down into itself. But when he sees me standing there, his face brightens. He's so grateful to see me, so relieved—and he immediately starts worrying that I've abandoned my important professional responsibilities to come.

A few minutes later, he gets up to go to the bathroom. I've seen him hobbling around the house for years now, and I'm used to frail—he's been juggling congestive heart failure, osteoporosis, cirrhosis, and about a half dozen other major illnesses for almost a decade. But now, the nurse takes one arm, and I take the other, and he leans over so far he's actually hanging by his arms, chest nearly parallel to the floor. He goes three steps and pauses, rests against the bureau, then takes five more steps and rests again. Glancing sideways, I see gray in his cheeks, a whitish gray like dirty marble.

He makes us wait outside the bathroom. He won't be helped in there. So we stand right outside the door, and when the toilet flushes I peek in and see him shuffle to the sink. He's wearing blue pajamas with a tissue folded into the breast pocket like a pocket square. He leans down with his elbows hard against the yellow tiles and washes his hands. On his way out, he stops to put the toilet seat down.

My father was a spy, a high-ranking member of the CIA, one of those idealistic men who came out of World War II determined to save the world from tyranny. Like so many of his colleagues, he ended up bitter at a world that mocked and frustrated and finally vilified him. His bitterness was the mystery of my childhood, turning me stubborn and defiant. Like most sons of unhappy fathers, I had a hole inside me cut to the shape of his sadness, a hole I tried to fill in all the usual ways and never did, because happiness would be too much of a betrayal. My miseries were a tribute to his own—a fucked-up gesture of fucked-up solidarity. So I was always leaving home and coming back and leaving again and coming back again, and often on these visits I would interview him, trying to bridge the gulf between us in the only way I knew. But whenever I pulled out my tape recorder, he would remind me that he had taken an oath of silence. That was always the first thing he said: "You know, son, I took an oath of silence."

\ \ \

In bed at night, he's wheezing and gasping so hard I think he's going to die with each breath. But he goes on as always, worrying about Mom and whether she's adequately covered by insurance and his pension, ground we've been over a million times before. He gives me advice on renting the house out after he dies. He philosophizes for my benefit, as he has all his long life.

"Accidents play such a large part in our lives," he says. "I don't mean accident like car accidents. If it hadn't been for the war, I would have had a very different life."

I've heard this a million times before.

Then he asks me if the doctor thinks this "slump" will get better. In my family we tell the truth, always have, sometimes more than we should, so I say I don't think it will. "There's always a chance, but I don't think so."

He seems relieved at that, seems to relax. Behind his breath, there's a rattle deep in his throat or deeper.

This life began eighty-four years ago in Burma. His father was a wildcat oil engineer from Louisiana (a proud man's way of saying he learned his trade on the job), and his mother was a tough Texas farm girl named Annie Strelsky—Dad never knew if she was Jewish or Polish or Russian and always told me it didn't matter because we were Americans. After the Burma oil boom ended, they moved to Whittier, California, a Quaker town surrounded by orange and lemon groves. Richard Nixon was one class ahead of my dad all through high school and college. Although Dad's parents seem to have been freethinkers— his father was a Freemason and fumed around the house about the night riders who attacked blacks moving into the area—Dad became pious at a young age, teaching Sunday school at a Baptist church. He studied Greek and Latin and by high school graduation could read Cicero in the original. At fourteen, he saw his father die, and he would remember until the day of his own death the sound of his father's last cry and the sight of his body giving one last jerk on the bed. Around that time, he discovered Will Durant's books on philosophy and plunged into study so deeply that within a few years, he suffered some kind of library-induced nervous breakdown and lost his faith in God.

So he transferred from Whittier to Berkeley and the Romantic poets—his letters home mention Pater, Shelley, Keats, Byron, Wordsworth, and Swinburne. He began wearing a "flowing, multicolored tie." He tried to join the Communist party, but they wouldn't have him. He swore to live the life of the mind at whatever cost. "Most of us are satisfied with too little," he wrote a friend, "and we never live even though we think that we do. We're pygmies, we're all the hateful, disgusting things that Swift said that we were, and the damnable thing about it all is that we seem complacently, oily content about the whole matter. By the Lord I'll escape this pygmy state if I have to spend the rest of my life doing it!"

After finishing his degree, he went to Paris, where he studied at the Sorbonne and earned pocket money by cataloging the pornography library of a wealthy French homosexual. After a year of that, he bicycled around Ireland and moved to Germany to study at the University of Heidelberg, where he lived in a *kameradschaft* house with a group of athletic young men who tried to pump him with the glories of national socialism. From his letters home, I get the impression that he was attracted by their health and vigor, but then he saw Hitler speak and was so disturbed, he went back home to study sociology. As he told me years later, he felt that literature hadn't given him "the vocabulary" to argue with those vigorous young Germans. But then his younger brother died of a self-inflicted gunshot wound that was or was not suicide—Dad always believed it was—and Dad drifted through a teaching certificate and a year as an English teacher before moving to the University of Chicago to work on a PhD in anthropology. When the Japanese attacked Pearl Harbor, he tried to sign up right away, but his glasses got him listed 4F. In 1943, his mother died of cancer in his arms and the Army noticed he spoke French and German and asked if he'd mind "wandering the battlefields at night taking papers off of corpses"—which is when he began the long transformation from that romantic young boy in the flowing tie to the complicated and difficult and decent and cruel and tender man I knew as my father.

This afternoon, Dad's pulse goes down to fifty (from eighty), and he gasps down lungfuls of air with his head back and lips wide apart, like someone getting mouth-to-mouth. He starts complaining about pain in his chest and pain in his right arm, and then his face seems to slacken into a death mask, his lower lip retracting over his gums almost to the back of his tongue. The nurse shows me the pulse on the chart and goes to call the doctor. Then my sister and the nurse and I all sit around him, stroking him—something we learned from the nurse, a squat young woman whose inward calm is very soothing to us all. At first, I felt awkward about it, stroking his arm for a long time before I got up the nerve to take his hand. I can tell my sister, Jennifer, feels awkward about touching him, too. We are the kind of family that never touched until we said goodbye and then gave each other a hard and awkward hug.

Later, when Jennifer leaves and we are alone in the room, he apologizes. "I'm sorry this is taking so long."

We did not get along when I was a kid. He was distant and preoccupied, and I was (I am told) a natural-born smart-ass. By the time I turned fourteen, I was sneaking out to take drugs, shoplift, and commit acts of petty vandalism, which on at least one occasion prompted the intervention of the local constabulary. That was also the summer he told me he worked for the CIA, but I can't claim high political motives for my rebellion. The only possible connection is that in 1968 he was the kind of guy who would work for the CIA and I was the kind of guy who wanted to drop acid and listen to the *White Album* over and over. That summer, we moved to Korea, where he brooded on the world's most rigid totalitarian state (just twenty-six miles north of our house!) and I dated Korean bar girls and smoked bushels of dope. Military intelligence officers wrote reports on my activities and sent them to my father, who gave me lectures on being a "representative of my country." Which seemed rather comical to me, since all my fellow representatives were just as whacked as I was; my friend Adrienne had a habit of carving her arm with a razor, Karen was dabbling in heroin, and Peter dropped out of high school and into a reefer haze. So I would bait my father at dinner by defending communism—all your better hippies live on communes, don't they? He would get insanely angry, sputtering his way into a lecture on totalitarianism before leaving the table in disgust. Once, I called him paranoid and he exploded into the most gratifyingly paranoid rage I have ever seen. It all came to a boil the day I got beat up by an MP—he called me a girl; I gave him the finger—who charged me with the crime he had committed, assault. When Dad came to get me with his chauffeur and his big black car, he took me to the office of the army general in charge of all Korea and made me apologize for forcing that poor MP to beat me with his club. Not long after that, those helpful men at military intelligence sent Dad a note saying I was a "known user of LSD," and then the army psychiatrists had a crack at me, and before long I was on a plane back to the States—sixteen years old and on my own. If I couldn't get into a college early, I was going to have to support myself. Thanks a lot, Dad. And fuck you very much.

The nurse keeps examining Dad's fingertips, which are turning blue. This is a bad sign. She takes his pulse and goes to call the doctor. Meanwhile, Dad keeps asking the time, which seems ominously significant. Then he keeps trying to tell us something, and Jennifer and I sit close on the edge of the bed, convinced that these are his last words. "Gee fi ohf," he says. "Gee fof."

Finally, I figure it out. He's trying to say G505—the satellite setting for the *Evans and Novak* show.

"We're here with you," I say.

He smiles sweetly.

In Italy, Dad spent his time rounding up spies with his two best friends, Gordon Messing ("the sloppiest soldier in the U. S. armed forces") and Gordon Mason ("handsome, debonair, witty, sardonic, a great lover"). He also fell in love for the first time, with an Italian baroness whose husband was a fascist officer. And managed to stop an antifascist riot in a small mountain town by climbing onto the hood of his jeep and lecturing the mob on "Aristotle's iron law of politics, to the effect that the anarchy and lawlessness of violence leads to tyranny." But by the end of the war, his romanticism had burned off completely. A letter he wrote to a high school friend shows him changed right down to the rhythms of his prose: "I feel older than the three years would have normally caused, sadder and very tired. I drank hard, played poker and shot craps, made love indiscriminately like all soldiers do. In three years I have hardly read a book, and feel now almost too restless to spend a single evening at home."

Transferred to Salzburg, Dad began arresting Nazis at the rate of fifty a month. (Later, the Austrian Ministry of the Interior officially declared his county "the best and most thoroughly de-Nazified county in all of Austria.") After each conviction, he sat his prisoner down in his office and handed him a scrapbook he had compiled of magazine photos of the camps at Auschwitz and Buchenwald. "I had come to hate the Nazi system," he wrote me years later, "and I mean hate it emotionally as well as intellectually. You will remember that when you were a boy, I took you to the Jefferson Memorial in Washington and asked you to remember the words he wrote, carved out above his statue: 'I have sworn upon the altar of God eternal hostility against every form of tyranny over the mind of man.' No better sentence has been written in the English language."

One day, a Soviet official came to Dad's office to bluster against America's recent refusal to repatriate White Russians to Soviet camps, shouting at Dad in "a bullying, overbearing manner, typical of the Soviet style." When Dad lost his patience and threatened to have the MPs drag him away, the official's attitude immediately changed to wheedling conciliation. That made a big impression. "All subsequent experience has convinced me that you can deal with the Communists and the Nazis of this world—and all bullyboy types—only from a position of strength. Their basic human philosophy, if you can call it human, is that of the bully—despise and abuse weakness, defer to strength."

Dad never stops giving me instructions. The doctor told him that fruit is good for you, and he wants me to know, too. "Remember that, son—fruit is good for you." He gets obsessed with a lost pill; it was in his bedclothes, he keeps saying. Did he drop it? Did he forget to take it? Should he take another one? A minute later, he worries if the nurse has taken a lunch break. I send her off and help him to the bathroom, and when I hear the flush, I open the door a crack and see him leaning over to wipe off the edge of the toilet bowl. He apologizes for taking so long.

\ \ \

From Salzburg, Dad went to Vienna. Those were the *Third Man* years, when Vienna was a free-for-all of spies, smugglers, and escaping Russian royalists. The Soviets were rushing into the vacuum left by the Nazis, and their tactics were so brutal that despite the size of Dad's operation—two hundred agents covering half of Eastern Europe—spying on them proved bitterly difficult. Austrian agents often disappeared to firing squads or prison camps. One was stabbed and thrown off a train. Ever the scholar, Dad began reading anticommunist writers like George Orwell and Arthur Koestler. He bought complete sets of the works of Lenin and Marx (still in our library to this day). Years later, one of his colleagues told me that some CIA agents just wanted adventure, travel, notches on the belt. Not Dad. "Your father *believed*," he said, with a lot of respect and maybe a bit of sadness.

As the forties came to a close, the revolution in China and the rumblings of war in Korea seemed to threaten fresh conflict, possibly even another world war. In 1950, a Soviet-inspired coup attempt in Austria sparked riots in several cities. In Vienna, the police almost lost control, and my mother and father—they had met and quickly married that year—were nearly trapped behind the Soviet lines. The atmosphere became so dangerous that Dad's bodyguard stayed at their home every night, sleeping at the foot of the stairs.

Dad wants to hear about the news. I tell him that yesterday they made peace in Ireland.

He's puzzled. "You're in denial?"

"No, Dad, peace in Ireland."

He still loves talking foreign policy, and when I read him the news summary from *Slate* magazine, he says he likes Netanyahu and feels the Israelis can't ever tolerate a Palestinian state.

"Do you think you could eat some Jell-O?" I ask.

He frowns again. "Time to go?"

Then to Athens, in those years one of the biggest CIA posts in the world. Dad and his agents ran operations against the Soviets from Kazakhstan to Hungary, including difficult targets like Bulgaria and Romania. They broadcast free-world news in fourteen languages, dropped leaflets all over Eastern Europe, maintained their own airport and air force of a half dozen planes and a few boats, too. Agent after agent disappeared into Albania, never to return. But Dad never told me about all this. It was Gordon Mason, Dad's old friend and chief of external operations of the Athens station, who finally filled me in. My complaints about the old man's stubborn reticence brought only a smile. "The chief of station in many ways outranks the ambassador in power—the number of people, the prestige, the money, the assets, the contacts," he told me. "Your father was involved in a lot of powerful dealings with a lot of powerful people in the world. But he never flaunted it. He was very modest. You look at him now, and you wonder at the power this man held in his lifetime."

He's too weak to wash his hands. I can tell it upsets him, so I wipe them with a wet washcloth and dry them with a towel. When we get back to the bed, I try to get him to sit up, which is better for his lungs, but he shakes his head. "Why do the so-called right things, when they'll just prolong this condition?"

He lies back, eyes closed, talking intermittently. Some of it is hard to follow. At one point, he says in a tone of surprise, "It's Jimmy Hoffa!"

I tease him. "So you're finally giving up the secrets!"

His eyes open, and he asks what I said. I repeat the whole exchange a couple of times until he understands. Then he gets somber. "It has always been off-limits for the agency to conduct domestic operations," he says.

Dad was ordered to Vietnam early in 1962. When he arrived, the war seemed to be going pretty well, and he plunged into work on the "strategic hamlet" program, a controversial series of armed settlements intended to slow the Vietcong infiltration. Four years in the Philippines had made him one of the CIA's most seasoned counterinsurgency specialists. He met weekly with Ngo Dinh Nhu, President Ngo Dinh Diem's intensely controversial brother. (Nhu later orchestrated the attacks on the rebellious Buddhists.) But toward the end of the year, the Vietcong began to win significant battles, and the Buddhist uprising began, at which point the American reporters on the scene began painting Diem as a paranoid autocrat who didn't have enough popular support to win the war—just another American puppet gone bad. The portrait was a gross simplification but had a pivotal effect on American policy: President Kennedy reacted by sending in a new ambassador, who treated Diem with undisguised contempt. That was Henry Cabot Lodge, still a controversial figure in my house—my mother loathes him. By the summer of 1963, Dad was a lonely figure in the Saigon embassy, the only ranking official who still supported Diem. As he often told me later, he admired Diem's courage and honesty and saw no "credible alternative" among the squabbling generals who would be king. By the time of Nhu's raids on the Buddhist pagodas, Dad was so linked to the Diem regime that he was suspected of complicity in the attacks. "That morning Richardson was a tired and shaken man," David Halberstam wrote in his first Vietnam book, *The Making of a Quagmire*. "He refuted the rumor immediately. 'It's not true,' he said. 'We just didn't know. We just didn't know, I can assure you.'"

Then Dad received a fateful cable from his superiors at the CIA. On orders from "the highest authority"—which Dad took to mean President Kennedy—he was instructed that unless he had "overwhelming objections," he was to support Ambassador Lodge and take the actions necessary to mount a coup. Reluctantly, Dad obeyed, sending the legendary CIA agent Lucien Conein (always "Lou" at my house) to encourage General Duong Van "Big" Minh, the primary coup plotter. On August 28, Dad sent a cable to CIA headquarters that later appeared in the Pentagon Papers, a cable he would come to regret: SITUATION HERE HAS REACHED POINT OF NO RETURN . . . WE ALL UNDERSTAND THAT THE EFFORT MUST SUCCEED AND THAT WHATEVER NEEDS TO BE DONE ON OUR PART MUST BE DONE.

The coup fizzled, and the *Times of Vietnam* ran a front-page story accusing Dad of trying to overthrow the government, which got him a place on the hotly rumored assassination lists. Meanwhile, someone began a behind-the-scenes campaign to get Dad fired. On October 2, the *Washington Daily News* ran a story by a Scripps Howard correspondent named Richard Starnes that accused Dad twice by name of disobeying direct orders from Lodge. The headline was "ARROGANT" CIA DISOBEYING ORDERS IN SO. VIET NAM. Citing a "very high United States source," Starnes called Dad's career in Vietnam "a dismal chronicle of bureaucratic arrogance, obstinate disregard of orders, and unrestrained thirst for power." Two days later, Halberstam corrected Starnes on the front page of the *New York Times*, writing that there was "no evidence that the CIA chief has directly countermanded any orders by the ambassador," but he also used Dad's name. "Outed" as a CIA agent, Dad was finished. A day later, he flew back to Washington, where the CIA hid him away for two weeks while newspapers all over the world ran stories about his ouster. The *Washington Evening Star* ran one of the few sympathetic takes: "The crime Mr. Richardson is said to have committed is truly fascinating. He is being charged in the bars of Saigon with declining to overthrow the government of South Viet Nam—incredibobble, as Pogo would say."

One month later, Diem and Nhu were deposed and shot to death, leaving my father with plenty of time to brood on the caveat the CIA chiefs had slipped into that fatal cable: "unless you have overwhelm-ing objections." In retrospect, it seems to have been put there just to give him something to torture himself with for the rest of his life.

Tonight I'm testing Dad's new painkillers. There's mariachi music next door, the jacarandas are in bloom, and Dad's blood pressure just plunged from one hundred over sixty to eighty over fifty. He sees Jen-nifer in the hall and doesn't seem to recognize her. "There's the lady who is going to give me my Metamucil," he says. But he still puts on his slippers every time he goes to the bathroom, and he still insists on having a napkin folded into the pocket of his pajamas.

Lying back on the bed with his eyes closed, he asks me: "When did this happen and how? This condition?"

I don't know what to say.

He turns to my mother: "I'm sorry to be such a problem."

"You're not a problem to me," she answers.

"That's important," he says.

I was nine and ten in Vietnam. I remember a French school with chickens in the yard, and Buddhist monks exorcising our house, and the morning I sneaked past the guards at the gate of our house to go to the marketplace. I remember chasing a girl around a schoolyard, trying to untie the ribbon of her dress. I don't remember the day my sister was watching a Disney movie in a local theater and bombs ex-ploded in the lobby, or the day our nanny foiled a kidnapping attempt by hitting a cabdriver with her umbrella and hustling my sister and me out of the cab, or the day one of the kids at my school tried to imi-tate the Buddhist suicides by pouring gasoline on himself and lighting a match. But I do remember the day my dad didn't come home and my mom sat around without turning on the lights and I got shushed by the servants. Years later, I learned that his helicopter had been shot down in the jungle and she thought he was dead.

Dad tells me that he's been hearing music—emotional music, orchestral, like a movie score. But there is no music playing. A day later, he says he's figured out where the music is coming from. "This music—it's produced by us," he says. "It's a subsidiary of ours."

Later, he murmurs: "Yeah, this is the tail end." He looks at me. "I hope this never happens to you—to be partly killed."

Later still, he frowns, puzzled: "This seems to be just a fragment of me," he says.

Most of Dad's stories are self-deprecating. Talking about Vienna, he tells me not about how powerful he was but about mistakes he made. One time, he was crossing through the Soviet zone and absentmindedly left maps on the backseat detailing the location of military forces in Yugoslavia. Along the way, he gave a young Pole a ride, and when they got to the checkpoint, the Russians became very suspicious and arrested the Pole. "They didn't touch the maps, which would have shown me to be a goddamned spy," Dad told me once, giving me his look of mock alarm. "If they had looked at the maps, I might not be here talking to you."

Years later, an officer of Dad's named Bill Hood centered a spy novel called *Mole* on the Vienna station. Dad appears as the savvy, tough spymaster Joel Roberts. "After six years in Austria," Hood wrote, "Roberts knew every alley in Vienna's *Innere Stadt*." The book tells the true story of the first Soviet counterspy ever recruited by the U. S., but Dad's version of the story is pretty undramatic. "As I recall, he approached some American at his car, got in, and defected," Dad told me. "Later, he was uncovered by the Soviet service and I think executed."

But what about convincing him to go back? Wasn't that a big feather in your cloak?

"I suppose it was, but it was very accidental," he said. "I don't think we deserved any particular merit."

The next day, my sister comes running into the kitchen. Dad's in a lot of pain, wants a shot of something, wants us to take him to the hospital. "I think this is it," she says. But when I get the doctor on the phone, he tells me that once we go to a hospital they'll hook Dad up to machines and keep him alive as long as they can, no matter how vegetative he might get. None of us want that. We stall, and the crisis passes. Dad lies back with his eyes closed, talking out of dreams: "The CIA contact . . ."

I can't catch the rest.

After Vietnam, Dad got kicked upstairs to a desk job as director of training. He brooded and drank, had a heart attack, argued with his superiors about training methods. His friend Frank Wisner (a legendary CIA agent who played an unfortunate role in the Bay of Pigs fiasco) had a mental breakdown and committed suicide. And the war started going to hell, and the hippies started protesting, and, looking back on it now, I can see how it must have seemed bizarre to them, these idealistic men who were just trying to save the world. Suddenly, the very people they had sworn to protect despised them! Nobody cared that most of those CIA excesses were done under orders from American presidents, that it was really the sainted John F. Kennedy who spilled the blood that splashed on Dad. It didn't fit into the sixties script: The hard old men were the bad guys, and by repudiating them, America would somehow become innocent again.

One day, Dad got a letter from a Vietnamese colonel named Le Quang Tung, who had been the head of Nhu's notorious Special Forces troops, the ones that raided the Buddhist temples. Tung said he was facing a firing squad and wanted to apologize; he was sorry for believing the rumors about Dad and now knew that Dad had never wanted to support the coup.

Dad threw away the letter. A few years ago, I harassed him about it. Didn't he care about history?

He gave me a pitying smile. "I have a feeling history is a pretty vain thing," he said.

We watch sitcoms in the study, then talk. Dad's voice has become a whispery tissue. "I remember the old days in Vienna," he says. "Dean was the youngest major in the Army."

Dean is my uncle, another spy. He's an ocean away, also dying of cancer.

Then we watch *Spin City*, and Dad smiles all the way through it. When it's over, the nurse helps him to bed. "It was a good night," he says.

A few years ago, I had lunch in Georgetown with a couple of Dad's old CIA cronies, Bronson Tweedy and Dave Whipple. Both were age-spotted and bald, with a kind of merry irony. They remembered Dad as a compulsive coffee drinker who had "a slightly ponderous way of expressing himself," as a "tough guy" who took controversial stands. They said he was one of the best, a "pillar" of the clandestine services. They even remembered certain improbable nights in Vienna when he danced to gypsy music till dawn. Then I asked them if they knew why he was so depressed and bitter after Vietnam. At first, they talked about his clashes with the CIA hierarchy and his impolitic but apparently unyielding conviction that the best field agents should be rotated into teaching jobs (first I'd heard of that). Then Tweedy sighed. "One of the reasons was he knew he was serving in a losing war."

Whipple nodded slowly. "An awful lot of people were depressed then."

\ \ \

At ten this morning, Dad wakes out of a nap and calls for me. As I help him into the study, my sister goes to get herself breakfast, but Dad waves his hand. "I think she should be in on this," he says. Dad sits on his little Greek chair waiting. He's hooked up to an oxygen tank, breathing through thin plastic tubes. Every few minutes, he spits blood into a kidney-shaped dish, dabbing at his lips with a napkin.

Finally we're all ready, and he begins. "I feel we're not making any progress," he says. "I feel . . . *I* feel"—he jabs a finger at his chest—"that this could just go on and on. So I want you to call Mike and talk to him."

Mike is his doctor. What Dad means is that he wants me to talk to Mike about giving him some kind of suicide shot. Dad pauses to spit into the dish, and I carry it to the bathroom and wash it out, trying not to look at the bloody phlegm.

"I suppose I could go off the machine," he says, meaning the oxygen. I look over at my mother. As it happens, this very morning a friend of hers sent over some morphine left over from the death of her own husband. I tell Dad about this and say we could always put a batch of it by his bedside if he wants. When he frowns, I try to reassure him, because I know exactly what he's thinking. "It's not like your brother," I say.

"I've always felt bad about my brother's suicide," he says. "I wouldn't want the grandchildren to think their grandfather did that."

"You put up a great fight for eighty-four years, Dad," I say. "It's not like you're taking the easy way out."

My mother and my sister are weeping. The maid vacuums in the hallway.

"I know you feel like it's dragging on," I continue, "but the doctors say it'll just be a week or two more. You're not in pain, your brain is still sharp—and Clinton still hasn't been booted out of office. Why not let nature take its course?"

He seems pleased by that. "Just a week or two?" he says.

I nod.

"And if you start to suffer or just feel you have reached the end of your rope, then know that we do have this alternative," I say. "Talk to me. You don't have to tell Jennifer or Mom. Just come to me."

"OK, then, we'll wait one more week."

Then we talk about dosage and doctors and make a few terrible jokes about Christianity while my mother and my sister weep nonstop.

"Well that's it, then," Dad finally says. "I think we've covered it all."

But I want to add something. "Dad, I just want to say, I admire you for looking at this straight in the eyes."

He seems very pleased by that. "All right then," he says, with a bit of the old authority. "Go on to what you were doing."

The early years of retirement were the bad years, when Dad earned his cirrhosis bruises. When the dark mood took him, he'd fasten on his completely imaginary money problems or some social error—he was obsessed with politeness to strangers—and pick at it until we were all bloody.

On one binge, he started talking about the Diem coup. He told me that obeying Kennedy's order was the biggest regret of his life. So drunk by then that he may have even cried a little, he said that he wished he had resigned instead of obeying that order. But it came from the president of the United States of America, dammit, with that terrible caveat.

Digging around in my mother's desk a few years ago, I found a series of cryptic notes in my father's handwriting. "Framework of guerrilla war," they began. "Operational involvement vs. analytic detachment. Colby & light at the end of the tunnel. Abandonment of Meos— 80,000—one of keenest pangs of defeat—fate of those allied with us. Nat'l interest—cold blooded. Cut our losses but written in human blood."

At the end of these notes, under the heading "Worst episode of my CIA service," I found this:

"Why didn't I protest more?
Machine gunner image—carrying out orders mentality
Highest authority and centralized information and judgement
Excessive modesty
Pension?
Conclusion—lack of sufficient conviction in thesis that Diem was indispensable."

After finding these notes, I asked my father what they meant. "I was probably thinking about that cable that said, Unless you have *overriding objections* to the decision of the president, you should carry out the coup plans," he told me.

And the line about excessive modesty?

"I don't have any comment on that."

Pension?

"That was probably a crude self-interest consideration," he said. "I suppose self-interest plays a role in most people's decisions."

I told him I doubted it played a role in his.

"Have it your way," he said.

Late that night, about two, Dad wanders into the study where I am sleeping and asks, "What do you call those pills?"

"Morphine," I say.

Once, about a year ago, I reminded him that President Kennedy praised him on his fiftieth birthday.

"Kennedy praised me on my birthday?"

I had the quote right there and read it to him. "I know that the transfer of Mr. John Richardson, who is a very dedicated public servant, has led to surmises, but I can just assure you flatly that the CIA has not carried out independent activities but has operated under close control of the Director of Central Intelligence, operating with the cooperation of the National Security Council and under my instructions."

Dad frowned. "I don't remember Kennedy praising me," he said.

"It was on the front page of the *New York Times*," I told him.

He shook his head and shrugged. "I don't remember."

Dad hasn't eaten for three days. The guy who runs the nursing service suggests a synthetic-morphine drip (Mexico forbids real morphine out of deference to the U. S. drug obsession), so I get Dad's doctor on the phone, and he agrees to write the prescription for this packet that Dad can carry around with him like a cassette recorder. They stick a needle into his belly to start the drip. An hour later, Dad goes into the bathroom and tries to rip it out. I try to convince him to leave it in, and he stands there, his pants around his ankles, saying he just doesn't like it and doesn't want to be hooked up to anything and just doesn't like it, dammit. My mother reminds him how he hated the oxygen mask at first and how he fought the catheter when he needed that last year, and finally he gives in and sits watching *Crossfire*. But as the day goes on, he gets more befuddled and scared. I hate what this is doing to his dignity.

I get angry at the bullshit media cartoons of cold-blooded CIA agents. I'm still annoyed with Don DeLillo because he told an interviewer that the real CIA wasn't as interesting to him as the idea of the CIA as one of the "churches that hold the final secrets," like it's all just a metaphor for the amusement of pretentious novelists. Other countries don't do this. We don't do it with Army Intelligence or the NSA or the FBI. But onto the CIA, we project all our anxieties about being grown-ups in an ugly world. And it's so easy to point the finger. So easy to sit in an office and write critiques. What's not easy is to choose between the possibility of a global gulag and the lives of thousands of innocent Vietnamese or Guatemalans or Nicaraguans and then to live with that choice—alone, as my father did. And on pile the critics with political motives of their own, which makes them just as dirty as the people who actually take action without the accompanying tragic knowledge, so they gas on and on about poor Salvador Allende because they like those Chilean folk-singers, dammit, but Diem—well, hell, wasn't he a bad guy? Didn't he deserve to die? And if I seem a little intemperate about it right now, it's because the *New York Times* fought this gutless paper war right down to my father's obituary, finding some asshole journalist who would say that Dad was sort of a good guy after all because he changed his mind about Vietnam—changed it to agree with the *New York Times*!—even though I told the fucking obit writer over and over that I didn't think he ever really changed his mind, except briefly in a moment of great pressure that he spent the rest of his life regretting. Fucking assholes.

He sits in the study with the oxygen tube wrapped from nose to tonsure like Salvador Dalí's mustache, and he raises three fingers. "What is that?" he asks.

"It's the morphine, Dad," I say.

This is our new secret code.

Then he starts joking around about turning his back on our cat, which has a vicious streak, giving us that goofy old look of mock alarm—a face I now make to my own kids. "You've still got your sense of humor," I say.

He smiles. "Two things, son," he says. "The first is humor, and the second is courage. I'd like you to tell the grandchildren."

He smiles at the nurse, his face in profile so thin and noble. I want to draw him, to take a photo, to keep this moment somehow. Then Mom comes in and leans down for a kiss. "Long voyage," he says, smiling at her with those bright beady death eyes.

When I was reading up on the old man, I came across a cable written by David Halberstam to his editors at the *New York Times*, dismissing the work of a reporter who'd written articles defending the Diem government. She spent most of her time interviewing head of cia bracket now thoroughly discredited unbracket . . .

In bed a few hours later, I couldn't sleep. Thoroughly discredited? What an arrogant jerk Halberstam was! The fucking guy was sneering at my dad two days after he landed in Saigon! I'm not making this up. It's in his book—two days off the plane, and he thought he knew more about Vietnam than the head of the fucking CIA!

Until that moment, I didn't realize how much I wanted Dad to be right—about Diem, about communism, about everything. It's odd, given how hard I rebelled against him myself. Not to speak of my left-of-center liberal-Democrat politics. What do I care about Ngo Dinh Diem?

At 3:30, we finish watching a movie called *Fly Away Home*. It's about a kid who learns to fly a plane so she can lead a flock of lost geese to Florida. My sister and mother and I all weep through the last half hour, and Dad smiles in perfect Buddhist happiness. When the credits roll, I smile at him. "You liked it," I say.

"*Loved* it," he says.

Then he sits across from me in his slippers and blue plaid pajamas, reading the paper. He doesn't want to take a nap. "At this point, I take nothing for granted," he whispers.

Halberstam, that asshole, trashed my old man again in 1971. This time, it was in an article for *Playboy*, and without the restraints imposed by the *Times*: "I did not think of J. R. as being a representative of a democracy. He was a private man, responsible to no constituency. Later, I was to think of him as being more representative of America than I wanted, in that he held power, manipulated it, had great money to spend—all virtually unchecked by the public eye. J. R., of course, bristled over the problems of working for a democracy. He disliked the press intensely. It was all too open. How could one counter communism, which was J. R.'s mission—little black tricks that never worked, lots of intelligence (mostly lies) coming in from his agents—with a free press?"

Aside from the line about countering communism, not one word of this pompous shit is true.

Dad can't take a dump. He goes to the bathroom and sits and sits, and it's really hurting him. My sister suggests that this is because he hasn't eaten for four days, so Dad weighs death against constipation and finally decides to drink a protein shake and some prune juice.

The next day, he's still constipated. He wants to go to the hospital, but then decides he doesn't want to go to the hospital even more, so he drinks another shake and more prune juice and starts vomiting almost constantly, spitting up a foul mixture of shake and prune juice and phlegm. Carrying the kidney-shaped dish to the bathroom, I gag and almost vomit myself. I'm starting to hate that infernal little Frankenstein pacemaker that keeps ticking his heart over and over, no matter what the rest of him wants and needs. I can see it under the mottled skin on his chest, hard and round like a hockey puck. Sometimes we joke about passing a magnet over it and putting him out of our misery. Dad nods out, forgets what he's saying, vomits again. Meanwhile, the TV news prattles on and on in the background like an evil guest who won't go away.

Once, I called the CIA public-information office and asked if I could see the old man's personnel records. CIA kids do stuff like this—one (who became a producer for *Unsolved Mysteries*) actually sued the agency under the Freedom of Information Act. A pleasant man named Dennis Klauer called me back with the official response: "Not only no, but hell no—and if you pursue this, we must contact John Richardson Sr. and remind him of his secrecy oath."

At around noon, he says he wants to have another talk, so we gather in the study, and he says pitifully, "My bowels have shut down."

The idiot blathering of CNN continues, distracting him for a moment.

"And something else—what else has shut down? My intestines?"

We turn the sound down and try again.

"Your lungs, you said."

"Yes."

Then the dog starts digging in the trash can, and my mom starts fretting, and my sister says she'll go get the garbage can from the guesthouse, because that one has a lid.

"I wish there was a lid for me," Dad says.

"That's pretty funny, Dad."

"Do you think there's a lid for me?" he asks.

I raise my hands to the heavens, taking the question for whimsy. But he persists.

"Do you think a doctor would do it?"

"What, Dad?"

He dips his head, his eyes going confidential. "Give me a lid for me."

It's odd how very old people get childlike when they tell a secret. For a second, I feel older than he is, and I lean forward and put my hand on his knee. "I don't think a doctor will," I say.

Then he nods so wearily that we try again to convince him to go to bed. But he won't. Never would, never will. Back in the binge days, I would see him walking to the kitchen at dawn with his tequila glass in hand. Sometimes he dropped it, and we would find the bloody footprints later. Now, when his hand droops, I try to pry loose the prune-juice glass without waking him, and he jerks back like I'm trying to steal it. Finally he drinks it down and I say, "As always, Dad, you drank it to the last drop." And I can't help feeling proud of him.

In the kitchen, my mother and I marvel over how tough he is. "It's a lesson in tenacity for me," I say. And she says, "It's a lesson for me that I won't go through that. I'll have my bottle of pills." And I put my hand on her neck and rub, and she shakes it off. "Don't do that!"

I went to his high school once, looked through his old yearbook. There was Richard Nixon looking like a young Richard Nixon. And there was Dad in a basketball uniform. He played on the varsity, never told me. The caption on the photo seems right to me even now: "Never flashy, but always in the thick of the battle, he proved in satisfactory manner to be a very capable guard."

Mom in bed. I say it's getting to be so hard on him. She says it's hard on us, too. Which is a sentiment worth honoring, I think. Weeping, she says she didn't think he'd wake up this morning, talks about maybe calling the doctor. A doctor put her friend Mary to sleep and would wake her up every few days to see if she was still in agony and finally just stopped feeding her through the tube. Maybe Mike would put a lid on him like he asked, put him in a deep sleep. Jennifer says the vet would be the best, and we laugh. And I think, Maybe it's up to me now. Maybe I should just do it and spare them the choice. So I go on the Internet and search for the Hemlock Society and discover it's all philosophy. "Where's the fucking how-to section!" I say.

Jennifer laughs. She's looking over my shoulder. "It's ridiculous," she says. "If you search for *terrorist handbook*, they'll tell you how to make a pipe bomb."

"Maybe we can use a pipe bomb?"

"Might not work," she says. "He's pretty tough."

When I was twelve, the headmaster of my prep school wrote my dad a letter outlining my many flaws. I found it in my mother's papers a few years ago, furiously underlined by my old man: "His homework shows superficial, if any, preparation. He gives little thought to neatness or accuracy. He does not appear to possess the willingness to apply himself to the task at hand."

This morning, he finally took a dump. He feels much better. But he's so tired he didn't even watch the news, and when he goes to the bathroom again, he asks me to come in with him. Leaning on the edge of the sink, head hanging, he says very emphatically: "Remember—this—is—lung—cancer." When he's finished, I pull up his pants. I see his withered haunches. The pillow-damp hair is stuck wild to his head. But weak as he is, he still insists on washing his hands, leaning over the sink with his elbows on the tiles.

When I was thirteen, he took me on this trout-fishing trip to Nova Scotia. He was a big trout fisher when he was a young guy. I remember it as awkward and dull. We heard the same songs over and over on the radio: "Crimson and Clover," "I Think We're Alone Now," "Happy Together." He stopped the car a lot to pee—from booze, I assume.

I call home, and my youngest daughter says she's fallen in love with a book called *Ella Enchanted*. She loves it so much she took it to a slumber party and read it while the other girls watched the Spice Girls movie. I tell this to Dad. "That makes me very happy," he says. "I couldn't be happier. Tell her I said that."

He's peaceful tonight. Lies quietly, rises only to drink milk or medicine. Asleep at nine. I think the end is coming soon.

When I was fifteen, he started leaving books on my bed: *Waiting for Godot*, *The Trial*, Albert Camus's *Notebooks*. They changed my life, but we never discussed them. He just left them and never said a word.

In the bathroom, he sits on the toilet for twenty minutes. I sit in a plastic chair across from him. The bathroom is all yellow. There's a black-ink drawing of a rearing horse on the wall above him. I can tell he's thinking deeply about something, and finally he says it. "If—I—need—something, ask—your—mother—first. Because—we—have—the—past."

I want to be sure I know what he means. "If you need something specific, or anything?"

I have to repeat it a few times before he understands me.

"Anything," he finally says. "Because we have the past."

That night, I hear the nurse pounding on his back. He sits there gasping, head hanging, breathing the oxygen from the tubes. When he recovers, he says, "I can't take this anymore."

The nurse does everything she can to help him. It pisses me off. I point to the oxygen, to the pills. *"No está bien; está malo,"* I say in my mangled Spanish: It's not good; it's bad. *"El necesita morir."*

He needs to die.

At around four, he hisses out his frustration: "I—can't—die."

Looking at my father on his deathbed, I try to picture the romantic Berkeley boy who wore that "flowing, multicolored tie" and quoted Shelley. I'm so sorry I never met him. I used to be angry about it, but now I'm just sorry. And maybe a little bitter. And I don't know if Dad killed him out of shame or if he just held the knife straight while history pushed it in, but I do know that, as time passed, Dad replaced his doubts with convictions and became so absorbed in his war, he forgot that happiness was part of wisdom and that he owed it to himself and to his children to try and earn it. And that is a sad, sad thing. And a dangerous thing, too, because when you become too sure that life is a tragedy, then little by little you begin to accept tragedy, and finally something perverse in you even begins to invite it. But life is a tragedy, isn't it?

One last trip to the bathroom. Even now, he won't use the bedpan. The toilet paper roll is almost empty, and that's when he says his last words:

"Another roll."

I get one from the closet and hand it to him.

Back in his bedroom, he eases into sleep. As the dawn light rises in the window, his breathing starts to change. The agonizing long pauses when you think he's stopped, and then a gasp sucking the air back in for one more round. Long pause and gasp, long pause and gasp. It's horrible. There's something monstrous in those sucking gulps at air, something so hungry and automatic, like his self and will are just the creature of this tyrannical little spark of survivalist life that forces him to go on and on and on. Outside, the birds are twittering and then the church bells ring as they do every morning here in Mexico, rolling out into the still, suspended air. Then Dad calms. His breathing gets softer and shallower breath by breath, with no more gasps or gulps, until he's breathing so peacefully, so gently, just skimming off the thin air at the top of his lungs. I move up and sit on the edge of the bed. The bells are finished, and now the garbage trucks rumble by.

The breaths get shorter and shorter and then he just stops.

EATING WITH MY FATHER

by Tom Chiarella

Around the house, my dad was a brooding, intense guy. He glared. He shouted. At the end of a workday, standing at his rolltop desk, holding a sheaf of bills, looking over his shoulder at some disturbance in the living room, he flat-out scared me. But I loved eating with my dad. I would tell him anything when we ate. The guy was clear-eyed and wise over a bowl of soup.

During high school, we ate every Saturday at a restaurant high atop an office tower in Rochester, New York. I had to get there first, pick a booth by a north-facing window, leave room for him to sit on the left, and order two Tabs with lemon. Every major conversation I had with the guy during those years occurred in that booth, over lunch. I had quit football suddenly. I'd banged up the car. I'd been in a fight. I'd cashed out my savings bonds without telling him. I'd paid for a girlfriend's abortion. Through all this, we ate. In this way, we got through it. Food filled the silences. Onion soup. Escarole and beans. New potatoes flecked with skin. Spinach. Always spinach. T-bones. Hard rolls. French fries with grilled onions. Over time, my father told me his share, too: that he'd been married once before, that his new boss had refused to pay him for nearly a year, that his business seemed to be at an end. At these times, I could see that he was eating with a purpose: he ate like he meant it.

He had his quirks—he liked lemon wedges with his salad, he ate the tails of cooked shrimp, he despised the way I used butter—but he was not overly concerned with the rituals or compulsions of food. When he allowed himself to gravitate toward the comfort foods of an immigrant's childhood—tripe, chicken gizzards, even bone marrow—he amazed me. A proffered forkful of food from my dad was his way of teaching. He wanted me to try things, to open myself up beyond cheeseburgers and tuna melts. And I gave it a shot, because there in those booths with the food in front of us, my dad could be trusted. When we were eating, I discovered him to be more than what I thought he was: braver, tougher, more generous, and more exotic than anyone I knew. When he ate, I wanted to be him.

I'm almost fifty now. The last time I ate with my dad, he was living in a nursing home outside Albany. We sat in a big room, fluorescents and linoleum, full of skeletons, four to a table, eating tapioca out of paper cups. He was still brave about the food, although for different reasons. It was a struggle just to eat, for one thing—he did the best he could with a fork, and I fed him the rest. And the food wasn't that good, of course, though he seemed to like the cheesecake. Despite how it sounds, none of this was particularly sad, except that now he didn't talk while he ate. He couldn't. I tried talking for a while, but I could see it stressed him. So then I was quiet. Yes, that part was sad. My father had forgotten what food was for—what he and I used it for—and that was unbearable. Eventually, though, he looked up and said, "You would like the cheesecake." I nodded and went to get a piece, offered him some off my own fork, but he didn't want any more. He said, "Go on, try it." And he was right. It was good cheesecake, better than I thought it would be. It was delicious.

"You look good when you eat," my dad said. It was something he said sometimes. "You eat like you mean it."

MY FATHER'S MEMORIES

by Ron Reagan

I knew it would happen one day; I just didn't expect it to happen
so soon.

Late summer, 1995. My father and I were lounging, fittingly
enough, poolside at my parents' home in Los Angeles. He had recently
revealed publicly that he had been diagnosed with Alzheimer's disease, and his powers of recollection had begun to falter—imperceptibly
perhaps to strangers but more obviously to those who knew him best.
Across formerly clear skies, scraps of mist had begun to drift. Sometimes
they were blank patches, sometimes visitors from years past. Familiar
names went missing. Different decades tumbled together, producing
odd juxtapositions. A couple of minutes earlier, having ventured a few
laps, I had climbed out of the pool to join my father under a large umbrella. He had looked me up and down, then suggested, straight-faced,
that I try out for the Olympic swim team. I was thirty-seven years old.
But in his eyes, who knew? Some memories, though, are remarkably re-
silient. Old athletes—and I count my father in this category—frequently
reach back to long-ago moments of mastery or narrow defeat. I knew
where Dad was headed: down a well-worn path, back about twenty-five
years to one in a long series of good-natured physical contests we had

engaged in as I grew up, back to the moment of my first real triumph, a swimming race both of us had assumed he would win.

"You know what the difference was?"

Rhetorical question. I nodded. I knew.

The race had taken place in our backyard pool in Sacramento the summer I turned twelve. My father had reached the brink of sixty that year, so we were both at an age fraught with danger. I had only just realized that childhood as I had known it was coming to an end; Dad, though I couldn't have appreciated it at the time, must have been hearing the first whispers of mortality.

The pool itself was a rectangle maybe twenty-five yards long— roughly regulation short-course size—rimmed with decorative blue-green tile and coated with fiberglass, which made your skin itch if you spent a lot of time rolling around on the bottom of the deep end reen-acting episodes of *Sea Hunt*. There's no telling who challenged whom, but as was our custom, Dad and I lined up in the shallow end on oppo-site sides of a crescent of steps leading down into the water. My mother was enlisted as a starter's pistol: "On your marks. Get set. Go!"

I had never beaten my father in a swimming race or any athletic contest, as I recall. His philosophy regarding such matters he had made clear a few years before. Once past the age of sentience—sev-en or so in his reckoning—I would surely know if he was letting me win. This would, in turn, undermine any confidence I might have in a genuine victory achieved at a later date. How much later he never speculated, but I would guess he pictured a strapping college jock fi-nally getting the best of his gray-haired old man. A skinny preado-lescent was certainly not part of the plan. As we pushed off for our down-and-back race, I was under no particular pressure to perform, and after a few strokes, upon glancing over to his side of the pool, felt mildly surprised to discover we were dead even.

\ \ \

Now, your average smart-ass twelve-year-old might be undaunted by matching up with a man near hailing distance to a Social Security check, but my father was not your average almost-sixty-year-old. Born before World War I, he grew up long before gyms had sound systems and fancy machines. Weight training was a foreign idea. Yoga would have baffled him. Spandex was out of the question. Real men—men healthily invested in their physical prowess—simply led "vigorous" lives. To that end, Dad rode horses, chopped wood, pounded fence posts, and swam—swam fearlessly in ocean breakers and, at home, back and forth in our pool. These were not casual endeavors squeezed in occasionally between office hours. They occupied a more fundamental, if unforced, place in his life. He had an actor's concern for his appearance and an athlete's pride in the smooth grace of his body's mechanics. At nearly six two and 180 pounds, he was an admirable physical specimen. Though he was older than the other dads I knew by ten, fifteen, even twenty years (he was forty-seven when I was born), I could comfortably assume that he was more than a match for any of them. Gentle by nature, he was nevertheless the kind of man other men instinctively knew to let be. Well into his seventies, after years of relative inactivity behind a desk in the White House, he would retain the power to impress. Brian Mulroney, the former prime minister of Canada, reminiscing recently with my mother, recalled visiting him in the Oval Office. Upon leaving, he remembered, he had clasped my father's arm above the elbow. "My God," he said. "It felt like he was made of iron!"

Down the pool we went. Dad never claimed afterward to have been easing up that first lap, and as far as I could tell, we were both swimming as hard as we could. Incredibly to me, as we approached the end where we would turn and head back, the race was still neck and neck.

A year earlier, as a scrawny eleven-year-old, I had joined the local community swim team and performed without distinction. I mostly remember the overpowering reek of chlorine, the stinging eyes, and the embarrassing pink paisley Speedos we were made to wear. I never won a race, partly because I was competing at the bottom of my age group, but also because the public nature of the swim meets—crowds of shouting parents, the PA announcer—threw me. Swimming well requires relaxation. That's why you always see Olympic swimmers gyrating their arms and waggling their legs before a race. They're not pumping up; they're getting loose. Tighten up and you'll enjoy all the hydrodynamic efficiency of a cinder block. At the only meet my father attended, I stood on the block, heard my name announced, and watched a hundred pairs of eyes swivel from Dad to me and back again as a murmur passed through the crowd. The gun went off, and I hit the water like a bucket full of hammers.

But now I found myself in familiar waters. I had spent the whole long summer in our pool, practicing somersaults from the diving board, racing friends up and down, back and forth, for hours on end, skin gradually wrinkling, till I was called to dinner. I could swim three lengths of the pool underwater without coming up for air, ignoring the throbbing in my head and the tightness in my chest until it seemed my lungs would burst. Now there was no crowd of strangers with an unnatural (to me) interest in my performance. Just my own mother and father. And, frustrating as that previous summer's interlude had been, I had learned a few useful tricks, chief among them the flip turn.

Most people when swimming back and forth across a pool will, upon making the far side, reach out with one hand, grab on, and then pull their legs underneath them, the better to push off for the return trip. It's an easy, virtually instinctive action, but terribly inefficient if you're in a hurry. Competitive swimmers, as anyone who follows Olympic swimming events knows, somersault as they reach the wall, allowing them to turn and kick off in one fluid motion.

I had adopted this technique out of necessity and practiced it religiously. And so, as my father and I reached the far end of the pool, I had a secret weapon.

About four feet from the end, I ducked my head and rolled into my turn. This was not yet a foolproof maneuver, but something I could perform reasonably well about 75 percent of the time. The odds and perhaps a bit of luck were with me. As I felt both feet plant firmly on the wall, I stole a look in Dad's direction and saw him just reaching for the edge of the pool. Kicking off, I held my body as straight as a nail and arrowed under the water until my momentum began to ebb, then rose to the surface and pulled hard with my right arm, allowing myself a deep drag of air. With my face back in the water, I could see my father complete his turn. I was now a full body length ahead.

Dad could, of course, see me, too. He must have been surprised to find himself falling behind, and I can imagine the tingle of adrenaline as it pulsed through his arms and legs. This couldn't be happening. Not in a swimming contest.

My father came of age in a river town—Dixon, Illinois. From the ages of fifteen to twenty-one, he worked summers as a lifeguard at the town's beach on the Rock River, Lowell Park. It was a job he was grateful for in those early years of the Depression. An old photograph shows a tall, slim young man, deeply tanned, hair bleached halfway to blond, with long, smooth muscles beneath his singlet. He is not wearing his thick glasses. Extreme nearsightedness had always kept him off the baseball diamond and had limited his utility as a basketball and football player. But nobody sees well underwater. The river was a great equalizer, allowing his natural athletic gifts to find full expression. He was once, he told me, approached by an Olympic scout who invited him to work out with the team preparing for the '32 Games. He turned down the chance to match strokes with Buster Crabbe because he couldn't afford to pass up his summer pay. As far as I know, he still holds the record for swimming from the park to the river's far bank and back. During those seven summers, he saved seventy-seven people from drowning, marking each victory over the deceptively swift current by carving a notch on a beached log. He was a small-town hero. Water was his element.

It was not all suntans and hooking up behind the changing stalls, this lifeguarding job. Rivers are dangerous. Mix in people determined to drown themselves and the dangers increase exponentially. I'd heard the stories, often couched as lessons. A river may look placid and smooth on its surface as it meanders slowly between its banks, but beneath the skin it hides whirls and undertows, powerful currents that will sap the strength of the strongest swimmer. Water was, my father stressed, an element to be respected. He had learned early that the shortest route from bank to bank was never a straight line but a swooping upstream arc. Work with water, he advised all his children, never against it; water will always be stronger than you are.

People posed a different challenge. Women, he recalled, were always grateful to be rescued, and some, he knew, would deliberately stray too far toward the middle of the river for the opportunity to be rescued by him. Men, on the other hand, would generally offer thanks only at the urging of their girlfriends, and even then grudgingly. Would've been fine. Not really in trouble, but thanks anyway. As he told it, Dad would never really acknowledge these dissemblings but just nod and keep whittling a fresh notch in his log.

Toward the end of summer, brawny farm boys finished with the harvest would begin arriving at the park. Most rarely encountered water deeper than an irrigation ditch and would invariably underestimate the river's power. In the grip of the current, exhausted, they would go vertical and begin to struggle. Their frantic clawing would on occasion need to be subdued with a right cross to the jaw in order to effect a safe rescue. Then there was the blind man. He was a towering hulk of a fellow, and Dad had spotted him the moment he entered the park. How, he wondered, would he ever manage to pull such a man to safety once he started fighting for his life? Sure enough, away from the beach the man paddled and within minutes was swept into the middle of the river. A noise went up from the assembled bathers as his big arms began slapping ineffectually at the surface, but my father was already in the water. Swimming out, following the bobbing head downstream, he wondered whether this might be his last rescue attempt. Drowning people will literally grasp at straws, anything for a last breath of air. Sightless, confused, and fearing for his life, this man would lock the first thing that came to hand in a death grip. That first thing would be his rescuer. Dad imagined them in a grotesque embrace, rolling along the river bottom toward the next town downstream. But to his immense relief, when he finally reached the man and put a hand on his shoulder, the reaction was immediate and total compliance. Accustomed his whole life to being led by others, he associated human touch with safety and instantly relaxed.

Ten yards out and the white blur at my father's heels told me he was kicking furiously. But despite an early surge, he had not closed the gap. I felt a rush of pure exhilaration: I was going to win! You have to swim slow to swim fast. This is not the answer to a Zen koan, merely one of the paradoxes involved in propelling yourself through an alien medium. In past years, other races, I might have shortened my stroke, chopping at the water in an effort to reach the finish a bit quicker—a beginner's mistake. Now I did the opposite, reaching farther, pulling longer, and as a result sped up. Five yards; three feet; touch. Raising my head out of the water, I looked over just in time to see my father glide to the wall.

My mother had been standing at the side of the pool since we set off, rehearsing in her mind, I suppose, the little speech she would give me to soothe the sting of defeat: You nearly did it; you've really improved; maybe next year. Now, sucking air through a victorious grin, I looked at her face and saw something new, an expression I didn't recognize. There was happiness on my behalf, no doubt, but mixed with something else, something very much like sadness. She turned to my father, and he saw it, too. He didn't have to ask.

"Huh. Well, whattaya know?" When he looked in my direction, I was still wearing my thrill-of-victory smile. "Congratulations," he said. "That was a good swim."

Fathers and sons have been competing since before dirt and, I imagine, have always experienced the same conflicted emotions. There is little to add to this oedipal saga; it's an ancient story. For sons, there is the thrill of holding your own in the world of men. But the price paid is a heavy one. To claim your prize, you must vanquish the god of your childhood. The strongest man on earth, the dad who can whip all other dads, must be brought down, made ordinary and all too human. Fathers, however proud of their progeny's success, recognize this defeat as a small death, a painful step down a road with a certain end. My mother surely felt this, and as I returned to thrashing around in the deep end and my father climbed slowly out of the pool, I saw her approach with a towel and place it tenderly over his shoulders.

It wasn't till later that evening that the question arose: "Did you do one of those flip turns?"

Summer was nearly over. Through some sort of unspoken understanding, neither Dad nor I requested a rematch. Soon the weather would turn chill and I would be back in school. By the following summer, one year older and that much stronger, I would be out of reach. My father and I never raced again.

And that was nearly that. But four years later, there would be one final struggle, an epic arm wrestling match fought to a stalemate on the coral-colored shag of my parents' dressing room. My mother was reduced to the role of nervous spectator—there was no need for an official start, just a quick, synchronized one-two-three-go. In years past, these matches had followed a set routine: Dad would allow me to slowly push his arm over nearly horizontal, then recover to the vertical, where I would struggle to exhaustion before he gently vanquished me. This time, nobody was faking it.

Naturally, my father had an arm wrestling story. A few years earlier, as governor, he had traveled to Petaluma, California, for the World Arm Wrestling Championships. A photographer had posed him with one of the contenders as if they were competing. In the interest of realism—or perhaps out of sheer perversity—he then suggested they "y'know, go at it a little." Dad may have been overly enthusiastic. The following day, his office got a call from the competition. My father had broken the man's arm.

We would battle for several long minutes, faces inches apart, neither of us able to budge the other, till veins bulged and sweat ran into our eyes. I think we were both stunned at how ferociously we were fighting just to keep from being outdone. By this time, my mother had seen enough. "Stop it! Stop it!" The anxiety in her voice brought both of us up short. We agreed to call it a draw, and that was that. I can still see us sprawled on the rug, panting, in the afterglow of combat. Dad's face had a slightly surprised look. Truthfully, I felt a bit ashamed. I was old enough by then to grasp that continuing to push and challenge would verge on cruelty. There was no longer any point. It was over.

In years to come, neither my father nor I ever referred to our arm wrestling match. It may as well not have happened. Our earlier swimming race, however, attained an honored place in family lore. Again and again, the story would bubble up in conversation, usually at Dad's instigation. My victory was always gracefully acknowledged, and I always responded that I'd had a great teacher. But the flip turn, as it transpired, had become a useful, face-saving asterisk for Dad. Yes, I'd won, but by employing a technique not practiced in his day. Were it not for that . . . who knows?

That my father should have recalled our race with such clarity no longer surprises me. The unimaginable so easily becomes the unforgettable. Seemingly ageless, accustomed to prevailing over time and nature, Dad did not yet feel old enough that long-ago afternoon to be beaten up and down the pool by a son who was still too young. Over the years, my father and I had raced each other countless times; all but one run together in a blur. His loss, so unexpected for both of us, sealed our memory.

Late summer, 1995. Another pool. My father and I sat beneath the shade of our umbrella, squinting out into the afternoon light. Alzheimer's will have its inexorable way, and Dad seldom swam anymore. Now there was mostly the past, some of it fading, some not.

"It was your flip turn that did it. Till then, you know, we were even."

Watching the sun beat down on the water, casting its net of light over the bottom of the pool, I didn't bother to turn in his direction.

"Yes, we were even."

MY FATHER'S FASHION TIPS

by Tom Junod

First it was Lubriderm, what my father rubbed briskly between his palms and extended in glistening offering. "How about a bit of the Lube?" he'd say when I walked into his bathroom. I was, like, eight years old, or something, so I had no choice but to put my face in his shiny hands. Then, for a long time, it was Nivea. "How would you like a little . . . *Nivea*?" he'd ask, with his brown hands singing. Now it was baby oil. Now he was seventy-seven, and I was thirty-eight, and we were sharing a room in a hotel near the ocean. He was sitting in bed, and I was sitting on the floor. He poured the oil into his hands and whisked them together, with a sigh of friction, and applied the oil to his face. Then he said, "Here—rub a little baby oil into your kisser. If you want to stay young, you have to keep well lubricated."

"Baby oil? What happened to Nivea?"

"Too greasy. Baby oil soaks right in. It's the best thing for a man's face."

"Isn't baby oil just as greasy?"

My father raised a thick eyebrow. "Listen to me," he said. "Learn my secrets."

He held out the bottle. I held out my palm. "Good, good," he said.

"Rub it right in—right in . . ."

There were always secrets. You could not walk into my father's bathroom and not know there were secrets. Secrets of grooming, secrets of hygiene, secrets of preparation, secrets of the body itself— secrets and knowledge. First of all, he had a bathroom all to himself— his bathroom, Dad's bathroom. And he made it his, by virtue of what he put in it—his lotions, his sprays, his unguents, his astringents, his cleansers, his emollients, his creams, his gels, his deodorants, his perfume (yes, he used perfume, my father did, as his scent—Jean Naté eau de cologne—for he was, and is, as he will be the first to tell you, a *pioneer*, as well as a fine-smelling man), his soaps, his shampoos and his collection of black fine-tooth Ace combs, which for years I thought were custom-made, since that was his, Lou Junod's, nickname in the Army: Ace. He called these things, this mysterious array of applications, his "toiletries" and took them with him wherever he went, in a clanking case of soft beige leather made by the Koret handbag company of New York, and wherever he went, he used them to colonize *that* bathroom, to make *that* bathroom his own, whether it was in a hotel or someone's house—because "I need a place to put my toiletries." He has always been zealous in his hygiene, joyous in his ablutions, and if you want to know what I learned from him, what he taught me, we might as well start there, with what he never had to say: that fashion begins with the body and has as much to do with your nakedness as it does with your clothes, that style is the public face you put together in private, in secret, behind a door all your own.

I have a sense of style, I guess, but it is not like my father's—it is not earned, and consequently it is not unwavering, nor inerrant, nor over-bearing, nor constructed of equal parts maxim and stricture; it is not *certain*. It does not start in the morning, when I wake up, and end only at night, when I go to sleep. It is not my creation, nor does it create me; it is ancillary rather than central. I don't absolutely f'ing *live* it, is what I'm trying to say. I don't *put it on* every time I anoint myself with toilet water or stretch a sock to my knee or squeeze into a pair of black bikini underwear. Which is what my father did. Of course, when I was growing up, he tried as best he could to teach me what he knew, to *indoctrinate* me—hell, he couldn't resist, for no man can be as sure as my father is without being also relentlessly and reflexively prescriptive. He tried to pass on to me knowledge that had the whiff of secrets, secrets at once intimate and arcane, such as the time he taught me how to clean my navel with witch hazel. I was eighteen and about to go off to college, and so one day he summoned me into his bathroom. "Close the door," he said. "I have to ask you something."

"What, Dad?"

"Do you . . . clean your navel?"

"Uh, no."

"Well, you should. You're a man now, and you sweat, and sweat can collect in your navel and produce an odor that is very . . . offensive." Then: "This is witch hazel. It eliminates odors. This is a Q-Tip. To clean your navel, just dip the Q-Tip into the witch hazel and then swab the Q-Tip around your navel. For about thirty seconds. You don't have to do it every day, just once a week or so." He demonstrated the technique on himself, then handed me my own Q-Tip.

"But Dad, who is going to smell my navel?"

"You're going off to college, son. You're going to meet women. You never want to risk turning them off with an offensive odor."

I never did it—or, rather, I did it that one time and never again. I am a son who has squandered his inheritance, you see; I am incomplete in my knowledge and practice of matters hygienic and sartorial. And yet . . . I want to know, and that is why one weekend late last summer

I wound up staying with my father in a hotel room that smelled of salt water and mildew, with his bag of toiletries spilling out on the bed and a puddle of baby oil shimmering in my palm: for the blessing of his instruction, for the privilege of his secrets. He had always told me that a man is at the peak of his powers from his late thirties to his early fifties, when he has forced the world to hear his footsteps—that a man comes into the peak of his powers when he *has* power and the world at last bends to *him*. He never told me, however, that that power can be measured by the number of secrets a man knows and keeps, and that when it became *my* time to make the world heed my step, I would want to know *his* secrets, for the paradoxical purpose of safekeeping and promulgation. My father's fashion tips: I'd listened to them all my life, and now that I was finding myself living by them, I wanted to tell them to the world, if only to understand where in the hell he got them, if only to understand how someone like my father can come to *know*, without a moment of hesitation or a speck of doubt, that the turtleneck is the most flattering thing a man can wear.

1. THE TURTLENECK IS THE MOST FLATTERING THING A MAN CAN WEAR.

This is axiomatic, inflexible, and enduring. This is an article of faith and, as we shall see, the underpinning of a whole system of belief. Mention the word *turtleneck* to any of my college roommates, and they will say "the most flattering thing a man can wear." Mouth the phrase "the most flattering thing a man can wear," and they will say "the turtleneck." This is because my father was born to proselytize, and when he and my mother visited my college and took me and my friends out to dinner, he sought to convert to his cause not only me—as he has as long as I've been alive—but them as well. Those who wore turtlenecks that evening were commended; those who did not were instructed and cajoled. My father was declamatory in the cause of turtlenecks, and as often as possible he wore them himself. Indeed, this is my wife Janet's first glimpse of Lou Junod: We have sat next to each other, Janet and I, for five hours, as our bus bucked a snow-storm and made its way from a college town in upstate New York to a mall parking lot on Long Island. We have kissed, for the very first time, the night before. We have held hands covertly the entire trip, although she has not yet smelled my neglected navel. Our seats are in the back of the bus, and so we have to wait a long time before we can get out. When we finally reach the front, there is a man standing at the door. He is impatient. He is not standing in the polite semicircle that the other parents have formed outside the bus; indeed, he is try-ing to stick his face *inside* the bus, and so we have to wait a long time before we can get out. He is, however, oblivious to whatever confusion he causes, and his chin is held at an imperious tilt. Although snow falls heavily behind him, he has a very dark tan, and his face shines with steadfast lubrication. He is, by his own description, "not a hand-some man, but a very attractive one." He has a strong face: a large nose with a slight hook; thick eyebrows, nearly black; and eyes of pale, fiery green. He is about five ten and a half, or in his words, "six foot in shoes." He is wearing a leather windbreaker, unzipped, and a pair of beige pants, which he calls "camel," and a ribbed turtleneck, tight to his body and pale yellow. Over his heart dangles a set of gold dog tags—his name is on them—and on his left pinkie is a gold ring of dia-mond and black onyx. He does not wear a wedding band. "Where is he?" he is saying, theatrically, with a habit of elaborate enunciation that lingers lovingly upon every consonant. "Where is . . . my *son*?" Janet looks at him and then at me and says, "That's not . . . ?" I look at him and say, "Hi, Dad."

Now, the turtleneck in this scene may seem incidental—just another detail, in an accumulation of detail—rather than an organizing principle. Don't be fooled. Anytime my father wears a turtleneck, he is advancing a cause, and the cause is himself. That is what he means when he says that an article of clothing is "flattering." That is where his maxim extolling the turtleneck acquires its Euclidean certainty. The turtleneck is the most flattering thing a man can wear because it strips a man down to himself—because it forces a man to project himself. The turtleneck does not *decorate*, like at tie, or *augment*, like a sport coat, or in any way distract from what my father calls a man's "presentation"; rather, it fixes a man in sharp relief and puts his face on a pedestal—first literally, then figuratively. It is about isolation, the turtleneck is; it is about essences and first causes; it is about the body and the face, and that's *all* it's about; and when worn by Lou Junod, it is about Lou Junod. The turtleneck is the most flattering thing a man can wear, then, because it establishes the very *standard* for flattery in fashion, which is that nothing you wear should ever hide what you want to reveal, or reveal what you want to hide. This is the certainty from which all the other certainties proceed; this is why my father, never a religious man—indeed, a true and irrepressible pagan, literal in his worship of the sun—believes in turtlenecks more than he believes in God.

2. THERE IS NOTHING LIKE A FRESH BURN.

I do not know exactly what my father looks like, for I do not know what my father looks like without a suntan. I have never seen him pale or even sallow. He does not often use the word *suntan*, however because he has been going out in the sun for so long that he has as many words for suntan as Eskimos have for snow. There is, for instance, *color*, which he usually modifies with a diminutive and uses almost exclusively to entice and encourage his three children—my brother, my sister, and me—to "go outside, stick your face in the sun, and get a little color." There is also *glow*, which seems to mean the same thing as *color*, but which requires less of a commitment—as in, "Just a half hour! Just a half hour in the sun, and you'll get a little glow, and you'll look and feel terrific." But neither a little glow nor a little color can substitute for the nearly mystical properties of *a burn*. Indeed, a burn is such a powerful thing that my father never asks his children to get one. A burn is such a powerful thing that in order to get one for himself, my father concocted, in his bathroom, a tanning lotion of his own invention, composed of baby oil, iodine, and peroxide (a few years ago, he tried to improve upon it by adding a few drops of Jean Naté, "for the scent," and it exploded). A burn is such a powerful thing that my father went to great lengths to make sure the sun shone on him, all year round, and turned the world into his personal solarium. In November and December, when he went out on the road for weeks at a time to make a living selling handbags, he always ended his trip in Miami and stayed for a few extra days at the Fontainebleau or the Jockey Club, so that when he finally came home he would come home—and this is another of his Eskimo words—*black*. In January and February, he would dress in ski pants and a winter coat, cover himself with a blanket, and sit for hours on the white marble steps that led to the front door of our house on Long Island—steps that were built with their reflective qualities in mind— with a foil reflector in his gloved hands and his oiled face ablaze with winter light. (Me, freezing: "How's the sun, Dad?" He, with tanning goggles over his eyes: "Like *fire*.") In March or April, there was Florida again, or California, and in the summer there was our house in Westhampton Beach, where my father indulged his paganism to its fullest extent; where the ocean was "nectar of the gods"; where the black bikinis he usually wore under his trousers he now wore to the beach; where the reflector now on occasion surrounded his entire body, like some incandescent coffin; where the sound track was my father singing "Summer Wind" and tinkling the ice in his cocktails; where he wore straw fedoras and V-necked angora sweaters; where his sense of style seemed to stretch all the way to the sunset and his burn was forever fresh . . .

3. ALWAYS WEAR WHITE TO THE FACE.

It's gone now, that house—it's a goner. The ocean took it away, years ago, and now wind and sand blow through where it used to be, straight to the sea. I mean, there's *nothing* left—not even a spike of foundation, nor a snake of plumbing, nor a hank of wiring . . . not even ruins, to mark, in shadow, my father's empire of the sun. That's what we saw, when we drove out there last summer, my father and I, to Westhampton Beach, to 879 Dune Road—that there was nothing at all left to see. Still, we had to see it . . . and then we had to stay at a hotel called the Dune Deck because, say what you will about the Dune Deck, it's still standing. You have to give it that. Its paint is faded, and the planks of its eponymous deck are splintery and mossy, and its rooms smell like old water . . . but at least it is extant and ongoing, this place where my father went to practice the art of swank; where he took my beautiful mother, Fran, for dinner; where he always sported drinks for his pals; where the image I remember is him standing at the bar with a gin and tonic, wearing white jeans—which he called "white ducks"—and a sweater over a bare chest, whistling; where, in the summer, the great Teddy Wilson, from the Benny Goodman Trio, played piano; and where, once upon a time, my father stepped up to the mike to sing . . . at least it is still *around*, this place where Lou Junod was a star.

A star, yes—that's what my father was, because that's what he wanted to be . . . that's *all* he wanted to be. My father's stardom was unusual in that he didn't have to *do* anything to be a star, even though being a star was what he *worked* at, every day. For instance, my father was a singer without being a singer—without being a pro. A crooner, my dad was, steeped in standards, with a voice that—when it was on—could make you cry. He sang his way through World War II, with an Army big band, in a revue called "For Men Only," after he was twice wounded. He sang all over Europe. He sang in Paris. He sang in an after-hours club with the great swinging gypsy, Django Reinhardt, as his accompanist. He never really stopped singing, either, even when he came home, to my mother, to Brooklyn and then Long Island, and then to us—he used to sing at clubs in New York, at closing time. The Little Club, the Harwyn Club . . . Not for money—as far as I know, my father never made a dime from his voice—but to *put himself across.* And when he went to see Dean Martin and Jerry Lewis one night at the Copa and Dino passed the microphone around to patrons and asked them to sing a verse, my father was prepared: he took the microphone in hand and sang to such effect that Dean Martin had to take it back. "Hey," Dino said, his voice whittled down to a point of low warning. "Hey," he said, glaring at my father over his shoulder, with a squint, with a glance of sudden, alarmed appraisal, sparked by his knowledge that there was now another man in the room, and to this man attention must be paid.

It was this, more than anything else, that was the true measure of my father's stardom, especially in the absence of other, more reliable measures, such as box office returns or record sales or public acclaim: the response he elicited from other stars. See, in my father's stories—and my father is a man of many stories—he has many encounters with celebrities, and each of them ends in the exact same way: with the celebrity in some way *recognizing* my father, with the celebrity finally having to take my father *into account*. If the celebrity is a beautiful woman, she will inevitably end up being unable to take her eyes off him, as in, "I saw Ava Gardner at Bill Miller's Riviera, with Sinatra, and she couldn't take her eyes off your old man," or, "Elizabeth Taylor was there—she couldn't stop flirting with your father. It started getting embarrassing—*embarrassing*!" (My father, by the way, is swift and aphoristic in judgment of his peers, and also unsentimental, so that Ava Gardner, in addition to being a "big nympho," was "shorter than I expected—nothing much" and Elizabeth Taylor was "short and dumpy, with a little bit of a facial-hair problem.") And if the celebrity is a man . . . well, then, he can't take his eyes off my father, either, but his regard is sharper, much more complicated, especially if he is something of a kinsman to my father—a fellow traveler—and as such a potential rival, like Sinatra and Dean Martin. 1952: Sinatra is at the

Copa. Sinatra is, in my father's words, "flat on his ass," because of Ava, the nympho. He is drinking, and his voice is gone. He makes a request. " 'All or Nothing at All,' " he says. Sinatra shakes his head. " 'All . . . or Nothing . . . at All,' " my father says, commandingly, with his own exaggerated singer's diction. Sinatra touches his throat and looks at my father, imploringly, pitiably. "Too tough," he whispers, softly and hoarsely, before leaving the stage. "Too tough." 1957: My father goes to Vegas for the first time, in the year before my birth. He rents a convertible and drives across the Arizona desert with the top down, and by the time he gets there, he is, well, black and, of course, vibrant with the pulse of the elements themselves. He goes to a coffee shop, and Dean is there, and Dean *recognizes* him—a nod. And then the next day, my father goes down to the casino, to play at the blackjack table, and Dean walks over, tan like my father, but not of course *as* tan as my father, and asks the dealer to step aside. "Let me deal to him," Dean says (or maybe, preferably, "Let me deal to *him*"), and for the next twenty minutes, that's what he does—Dean Martin deals cards to Lou Junod. It's just the two of them, two men wearing suits and shirts with French cuffs at twelve o'clock noon, in the middle of the freaking desert, and somewhere along the line it must occur to them—well, at the very least, it occurs to my dad—that they are men who very easily could have lived each other's lives . . . which is why my father always told me never to ask for autographs ("They should be asking for *your* autograph") . . . and which, I suppose, is why, thirty-eight years later, when I was about to interview John Travolta, this was my father's advice: "Where are you staying? Do they have a pool? OK, this is what you do—listen to your father: this afternoon you go to the pool, and you get some goggles to cover your eyes, and you put your face in the sun, and tomorrow you wear white to the face and a nice tie, and you show John Travolta how good-looking you are."

Ah yes, of course—wear white to the face. A white shirt or a shirt with a white collar. Why? Because it's *flattering*, that's why. Because you can't wear a turtleneck all the time, or even a lot of the time—that's the tragedy of the turtlenecks—but you can always wear white to the face. And because when you wear white to the face, the light is always shining on you . . . As it is right now, at the Dune Deck—the sun is shining on my father. He is wearing a polo shirt and khaki shorts and Nike sneakers and white socks. He is retired and has been for nearly ten years. He has two major complaints, each of which is long-standing: one, that he is "shrinking," and two, that he is losing his hair, or rather, losing his hair at a race in excess of the rate at which he was losing his hair when he first started complaining about losing his hair, which was at the very least thirty-five years ago. We are drinking cocktails, and our faces are in the sun. "OK, Dad," I say, "what are some of the rules a man should remember when he's getting dressed?"

"Well, always try to wear white to the face," my father says automatically, repeating a motto, a chant, a mantra my brother, Michael, and I have heard, say a thousand times in the course of our lives, usually when we have worn something other than white to the face, and have been accused of thereby "disfiguring" ourselves. "Particularly if you're tan. Gray is the worst color you can wear. Don't ever wear a gray shirt. Gray or brown."

"I have a gray shirt," I say.

"You do? Never wear it." Then, after a moment's reflection, during which my father almost winces, in order to set his teeth for the impeccable rendering of his final judgment: *"Burn* it."

4. MAKE SURE TO SHOW PLENTY OF CUFF.

I bring a Calvin Klein blazer to the Dune Deck to wear at night, and when I show the jacket to my father, I make a confession: "Dad, I think the sleeves are a little long."

"Get them shortened immediately," my father says. "For chrissake. I can't stand long sleeves. Jesus Christ! Don't waste any time . . ."

They work, my father's fashion tips. That's what's funny about them, besides the fact that they are . . . well, funny in the first place. They work, or they worked, for him, for my father. They were cohesive and complementary; they spoke in a single voice; they were his manifesto. Take a look, for example, at a picture of my father standing in a group of his fellow salesmen at a bar mitzvah circa 1962. Take a look at the one man whose jacket sleeves cover his shirt cuffs, like the sleeves of a cassock. He does not look merely glum or sour; he looks defeated, whipped, *scared*, precancerous—a recessive man, with a receding hairline. Now take a look at my father, holding in one pinkie-ringed hand a drink *and* a cigarette. He is about forty-three years old, and, by God, he is *glistening*, for he is in his prime, and all the elements are in place. He has a fresh burn, and he is wearing a shirt with a high collar. He is wearing a suit of midnight blue, single-breasted, with a silver tie and a handkerchief in the pocket (I've never heard him call it a pocket square), which he does not fold into regimental points but rather simply "throws in there," so that what shows is just "a puff." He is undoubtedly wearing bikini underwear, for anybody who wears boxer shorts is "a square" or "a farmer," as in, "What are you, a farmer?"; and he is undoubtedly wearing socks, or "hose," that go "over the calf, knee-high," for if there's anything he hates more than long sleeves on a suit jacket, it's "ankle socks," because "I can't stand to see someone sitting down with their ankles showing—their white ankles and their black socks." His shirt has French cuffs, of course, and he's showing plenty of them—"at least an inch"—and he looks *sharp* . . . and by sharp I mean avid, by sharp I mean almost feral, by sharp I mean that if this were not a bar mitzvah but rather a meeting of the Five Families, the *schnorrer* in the long sleeves and the boxer shorts and the ankle socks would be the guy fingered for a rubout and the guy showing plenty of cuff would be the man commissioned for the kill. 1962: A good time for sharp dressers. 1962: Even the freaking *president* is a sharp dresser, and he's just about the same age as my father, and as for him, as for Lou Junod, well, he's still coming on, and if he looks, in this picture, slightly dangerous, in his own proud display, I also have no doubts that on this resplendent day he was one of the most beautiful men in the world.

"I didn't grow up with any advantages," my father says at the Dune Deck. "I didn't have any money; I didn't have any brains—all I had was my looks and my charisma." Yes, that's right: his fashion tips worked because they had to work—because he had nothing else. No education to speak of, and no religion worth naming; no father (his father was a briny, bingeing drunk, and whenever any of us mentioned him, whenever any of us used the words "your father," Dad was quick to correct us: "I *had* no father"); not even any history (to this day, I have no idea when my father's forebears came to this country or who they were or where they came from). He came out of nowhere, thirteen pounds at birth, born to a great, kindly, bawdy woman who played piano in the pits of silent-movie houses. So he was big from the start, Big Lou, but that's all he was, and so he had to just keep getting bigger—for my father, it was celebrity or bust. His mentors, his teachers, his influences—they weren't *men*; they were gorgeous silvered shadows, dancing across movie screens . . . and by the time he was sixteen or seventeen, he was singing their songs, blanching the Brooklyn from his voice on the way home from the theater, and he was dressing like them, or trying to, anyway, and so was everybody else. That's the most amazing thing about listening to my father's stories of his coming of age—the sheer aspiration in them, and how easily it was shared and passed around; the way so many of them begin with my father and one of his rivals squaring off for a fight over a girl and end with the two of them *recognizing* each other before they ever come to blows and then going off somewhere to talk about clothes, of all things, and about style, and about class, and to argue over who was the better dresser, Fred Astaire or Cary Grant or Walter Pidgeon. My father believed, absolutely, in the old saw, at once terrifying and liberating, that "clothes make the man," and so did his friends, and so everything they wore had to tell a story, and the story had to be about them, because otherwise, the world was never going to hear it. That's really my father's first fashion tip, come to think of it: that everything you wear has to add up, that everything has to make sense and absolutely f'ing *signify*. He did not come up in the current culture of corporate individualism, so he could not let himself off the hook by wearing some fucking T-shirt that says nike on the front or chicago bulls; he has never been able to understand the utility of dressing, intentionally, like a slob, nor to discern what preference a heterosexual man is advertising when he wears an earring. "What do they *mean*?" he asks of earrings. "I've asked, and I've never gotten a good answer. Do they mean that you're a *swinger*? Do they mean that you're *free*? Nobody's ever been able to tell me . . ."

Irony? Irony is no answer, because in my father's view, a man is not allowed irony in the wearing of clothes. Irony is for women, because for them clothes are all about *play*, all about tease and preamble—because for them dressing is all about undressing. For a man, though, clothes both determine and mark his place in the world; they are about coming *from* nakedness rather than going *to* it—and so irony spells diminution, because irony says that you don't mean it . . . and you *have* to mean it. You have to mean what you wear. Hell, my father remembers what he wore at just about every important moment in his life, and even at moments of no importance at all—moments whose only meaning derived from the fact that my father was wearing clothes worth remembering, moments when it might have seemed to my father that the clothes on his back and the sincere force with which he wore them were enough to deliver him where he wanted to go: "You know, I used to walk on a cloud when I walked down Fifth Avenue and went to La Grenouille for lunch. Like I *owned* it, you know? I remember one day I met [a fellow salesman, named Joel] with his wife. I was wearing a beige glen plaid suit—beautiful—and a shirt with a white collar, with a silk grenadine tie and a set of nice cuff links, and Joel's wife said, 'Joel, I never saw anything like it. Look at the way these women are carrying on over Lou. Every place we go. It's unbelievable.' And it was. It really was. And I used to feel so good, I couldn't believe it—and that was enough to satisfy me. I didn't have to go any further with it. And whatever aspirations I had of being theatrical, of being in show business, I *was*—I was."

5. THE BETTER YOU LOOK, THE MORE MONEY YOU MAKE.

There is a woman at the Dune Deck with a dark tan and long black hair and a block of brilliant white teeth. "My God," my father says, "what teeth! Those are the most beautiful teeth I've ever seen in the flesh." Now, I must say that I've heard this before, that this is not a particularly *unusual* utterance from the mouth of my father, because my father has a white fetish—as evidenced by his white cars, white pants, white collars, white marble steps, etc.—and on top of his white fetish he has a teeth fetish, so white teeth move him greatly, often in the direction of hyperbole, in regard to both women and men. For instance, a couple of years ago, I went to a baseball game in Atlanta with my parents and ran into a friend of mind named Vince. "My God, what teeth he had!" my father said when we got back to our seats. "Those are the most beautiful teeth I've ever seen in a man." He has also been known to ask, flat out, upon first meeting someone, "Are those your teeth? Jesus, if I'd had teeth like yours . . ."

My father does not have great teeth, nor do I. Oh sure, he has white teeth now, but as he says, "Those are all money; those are all work." Back when he was singing, he was very self-conscious about his dingy choppers, and he often wonders now whether his teeth were what prevented him from going as far as he could have gone in show business. And as for my teeth . . . well, I was sick a lot when I was a kid and ran a lot of fevers and took a lot of medicines, and so it's like someone lit a Magic Snake in my mouth—my teeth are an efflorescence of sulfur and carbon and ash. My mouth is forever in the shadows, and so it is no surprise to me, when we go back to our room at the hotel, my father and I, and lie together on his bed, staring at a ceiling slovenly with unsealed seams, that my father says, as he has said so many times before, "Do you mind if I ask you a question? You can tell me to mind my business, but when are you going to get your teeth fixed? What are you waiting for? You're in the entertainment business now, son—the *better* you look, the more *money* you make. Will you listen to your old man for once? The better you *look*, the more *money* you make. The better you look, the more money you make.

I don't tell him what I realize, at precisely this moment, in answer to his aphorism—that I have chosen to make a living out of printed words for the very purpose of *transcending* my dim teeth, my shadowed mouth. And I don't tell him, because for my father, there is no possibility of transcendence: He is attached to his teeth, and attached to his body, and attached to his clothes, in a way that I have never been attached to mine. He has nothing else now, except his family, which has become everything to him, while I have *this*, this urge not to sing but to somehow speak and *tell* . . . except that, of course, in the end writing is the same as wearing clothes: you do it to have some say over how you look to the world, and you wind up revealing precisely what you've hidden, and more than you will ever know.

"Dad, what's the best you've ever looked?" I ask him that night at dinner. "I mean, the *precise* moment when you looked your best." I figure that he will know the answer to this one. I figure that he will talk about the bar mitzvah in 1962, or walking down Fifth Avenue to La Grenouille, or coming down the stairs at El Morocco and feeling like "a bride at her wedding," or the night he sang to close a club in Dallas and Zsa Zsa Gabor danced in lonely circles in front of the microphone . . . I figure that there will be a single instant when the world opened up to him and that it will be emblazoned upon his memory. But, no—there is no single instant, and when my father answers my question, it is without hesitation: "The best I ever looked? Every day of my life.

People will think I'm crazy, but I mean it. I felt like a celebrity *every day of my life*. I looked so good, I never wanted to go to bed."

We have the best table in the house, at the restaurant located within the Dune Deck, which is named after its chef, Starr Boggs, and which, by the way, is excellent—or in my father's appraisal, *elegant*. We are sitting at a corner table, by a window through which you can see the black and white of the ocean and hear its yawn and sizzle and splat, and my father is wearing a yellow polo shirt, white ducks, brown loafers, and a white zippered windbreaker with epaulets. I am wearing khakis and a white dress shirt, with its collar unbuttoned, and the Calvin Klein blazer, which my father asked me not to wear when we were getting dressed for dinner: "You're not going to wear a jacket, are you? Aw, c'mon Tommy—I didn't pack one because I didn't think we'd *need* one. You're going to make me look bad." Then he went downstairs to get a drink at the bar before dinner, and as soon as he left the room I put the blazer on and didn't take it off. I wasn't trying to make my father look bad or show him up, but, hell, it was my genetic *destiny* to wear that jacket, and I was ready to claim it. And besides, I had a little glow, and I was wearing white to the face, and I left the cuffs of my shirt unbuttoned in order to show them off, and I have to admit that I looked *pretty fucking good*. "Look at you, you son of a bitch," my father said when I walked into the bar. "You look handsome—handsome! You see what a little color can do? But you have to work on it. You should forget that *natural* stuff and try to get a little sun whenever you can. That natural stuff doesn't cut it anymore—it's not very in . . ."

Does my father look handsome on this night, at the best table in the house? He does; he does, indeed. And now, to tell him so, here come the women. Or, I should say, the *woman*—in this case, a woman about my father's age, whose face is etched with lines of runic complexity and who is wearing a visor that says royal viking princess and enormous square eyeglasses and a white-on-blue polka-dotted jacket over a blue-on-white polka-dotted dress: a peppy, strapping old gal who limps over to our table on a four-pronged cane and says, "Tell me, did you two get the best table in the house because you're so good-looking, or do you know the owner?" Then she looks at my father and introduces herself: "Clara. Clara Straus. As in Johann . . ." Then she leaves, to no music, and we order our food, and when I choose our wine, my father—who is watching me, who is always watching—says, "You've got style, kid; you've got style." His eyes draw fire and color from drink, and now they focus, with an intense effrontery, on the table behind me. "There's an actress over there, and I forget her name. Begins with an *l*. Very famous." I turn around for a second and see a tiny, dark-haired woman with an even tinier head, a woman who is at once exquisite and insectoid, and who is so perfectly composed that she seems to turn all movement into a tremble.

"Susan Lucci," I say.

"That's right, that's right," my father says. "Is that her? Your mother doesn't like her, you know. Not a lot of women do. She's the kind of woman that men like and women don't."

Can she keep her eyes off my father? I don't know, because for the remainder of the meal, my back stays to her. But he can't keep his eyes off her, that's for sure, and at one point, he dips his chin, and as he scrutinizes her, he strikes a pose of suave regard.

"Dad, what are you doing?"

"Trying to catch her eye," he says.

"Well, is it working?"

"She's weakening, my son," my father says. "She's weakening."

We stay at the bar after we finish our meal because my father wants to drink grasshoppers ("You've *never* had a grasshopper? They were the *in* drink at one time") but mainly because he doesn't want the night to end. "I don't have to tell you how much this means to me," he says, with his brown, mottled hand around my wrist. "It's been a long time since I've been in a place like this—with a *crowd* like this." Yes, my father is part of the crowd again, part of the crowd of hustlers and jostlers and guys coming on, of cigar smokers and martini drinkers and a woman in a silvery blue cocktail dress who is, in my father's estimation, "stacked" . . . and so the lessons never stop. "Dad, what do you think about that guy turning up his collar under his blazer?" "Your father did that fifty years ago." "Dad, what do you think of band-collared shirts?" "I'd wear a band-collared shirt—to bed. They look like pajamas. The worst is when they're worn with tuxedos. I can't stand that. They look like the dirty undershirt Dean Martin wore in *Rio Bravo*."

He falls asleep, in his clothes, the moment we get back to the room. He snores, with his fingers folded on top of his navel, and I take off my shoes and walk down to the ocean, in my blazer and khakis, under a black seam that splits the spangled sky and vaults out into the ocean forever. The only excuse for a man to grow a beard is if he has a weak chin or acne—that's what I know from my father. Make sure to splash some cologne on your privates—that's another thing. Never wear navy blue and black—that's what I came to know on the morning of my wedding, when I wore a navy blue suit and black shoes, and my father said, "What are you—a policeman?" ("But Dad, what kind of shoes *should* you wear?" "With a navy blue suit? Navy blue shoes.") As for the rest . . . as for everything else . . . not what I know *from* him, but rather what I know *of* him—that's harder, of course, because, well, why do you wear clothes in the first place, if not to cover up? I mean, Adam and Eve found *that* out quick enough—that clothes are totems of simultaneous confession and disguise. They are masks that unmask you, and what I knew of my father, through his clothes, was this: That he was going out. That he was going away. That he was heading for Miami or Atlanta or Dallas . . . That he was dressing for *other people,* an audience somewhere; that he was dressing for Frank and Ava and Dino and Liz and Zsa Zsa; that he was dressing for the *world*; that he *belonged* to the world as much as he belonged to us, and we had to let him go. *Let him go*—that's what my mother always said when my father was going out, and a few months ago, when I visited one of our old next-door neighbors, this is what she told me: "I remember one day your father was flying south, and he had a black tan, and he was wearing a white Bill Blass jumpsuit with a zipper, and I said to myself, 'This is the most gorgeous creature I've ever seen.' And I said to your mother, 'Fran, are you going to let this man *out* like this?' And your mother said, 'Ah, let him go. Let him go.'"

And then he came back. He always came back, to tell us what he had seen and what he had *found out.* He always had news, my father did— he always had the scoop, about who had the smile, who had the hand- shake, who had the toupee. He always told me what I needed to know about the world . . . and the world told me what I needed to know about him—that, yes, indeed, he owned it. He was a *terror*, my father, when I was young—he was hell-bent on mastery, and for years I was afraid of him . . . the sheer booming size of him. Then, for a long time, I idolized him, until I realized, not very long ago, that I have spent my entire life moving toward him. See, my father doesn't belong to the world anymore—he's given it up, or it's given him up, or it's just flat gone, like our beach house down the road. His world is no bigger now than his family, and he doesn't even have to dress for it. But certain things still belong to *him*, and now, here I am, standing on the beach in the dark, with a seven hundred dollar jacket on my back and my trousers rolled and my father snoring back in the room, and I'm stepping into the ink of the ocean—because just as the ocean in Westhampton will always be *his*, his secrets will always be his secrets. Lou Junod: he was determined to make his mark, and God, he *did*, and now, as I walk into my life, I walk into his, into the gift he gave me, his first and final fashion tip: The knowledge that a man doesn't belong to anyone. That he belongs to his secrets. That his secrets belong to him.

CODA: FROM A
DAUGHTER

MY FATHER, THE BACHELOR

by Martha Sherrill

T here were a lot of women to call after he died. The old girl-friends I knew of, the ones in San Francisco, were easy to find. They were a part of my life I'd lost track of, like older sisters who'd gone away to college and never come back. They were all smart and gentle and kind. They were independent. They had big eyes, soft, curly hair, and slight overbites. They tended to be half Jewish—a particular taste of his. One of them I had begged him to marry. Only one of them I didn't approve of. And there's one—my father's art dealer—who swears she never slept with him, and I believe her, but she was definitely a girlfriend anyway. She came to the house a lot at the end—came to his sanctuary of glass at the top of the Marin Headlands—and always brought food and made him laugh, and I'd see them sitting up on the chairs in the living room, holding hands and looking out over Richardson Bay. It's always been hard to explain to people, but it wasn't just sex that my father was after—which is why the word *playboy* doesn't capture what he was exactly, or even *ladies' man*. It was women. My father loved women in every way and gener-ally in the plural.

Some were unknown to me, just entries in a slim black address book that he kept in his nightstand—women who'd moved away or married, women who weren't in touch anymore. I hadn't met them. I knew them only by the nicknames he gave them. There were Crazy Girl and Mrs. Wolfman and Madame X. (Later on, inexplicably, she became Stump Arms.) He had one called Neighbor Friend.

And there was Blue Icon. I had never met her, nor heard much about her until the last three years of his life. I was visiting one time, and he asked me to choose among several pictures of himself to send to "an old flame." He was sick by then, on oxygen at home and trying to conquer a disease called pulmonary fibrosis, a kind of slow leathering of the lungs. Blue Icon, he told me, was a girl he'd known as a boy growing up in San Marino, California. They had gotten back in touch after fifty years and had begun a correspondence. They'd fallen in love by letter, and then, after Blue Icon had a stroke and couldn't write, they had a phone relationship.

I had forgotten her nickname by the time he died—my brother and I spent a breakfast trying to remember it. After going over every page of the black address book four or five times, I noticed a blue sticky note with the scribbled word "Icon" and a phone number with a Santa Barbara area code, and I called it. A quiet voice answered the phone. "Hello?"

"Hello . . . this is Martha Sherrill. I'm the daughter of Peter Sherrill."

"Yes?"

"I've called to say that he died Wednesday morning."

"*Ohhh*...I was afraid of that."

We spoke of details, the wheres and hows of his death—it happened at home, with my brother, after only one night of not being able to breathe. I had a sense these were the kinds of things that girlfriends wanted to hear, as a way to feel they were with him, too, in the end. It wasn't so bad, I told her. He was lucky. He had always been lucky.

"I shall miss him very much."

"Me, too," I said.

"Who will I talk to now?"

"I know," I said. "I worry about that, too."

He called me every day for twenty years, sometimes more than once. It wasn't always convenient. It wasn't always compelling. He was a monologuist, a blabber, a man who had many words for his many interests. We talked about movies and about books we were reading. We talked about buildings we liked and paintings. We talked about whatever bad TV show he'd become hooked on. (In the last year, he was devoted to *Spin City*.) We talked about things I was writing—he always asked to hear the opening paragraphs. More often than not, though, he brought the conversation around to his favorite topics— the troubled career of tennis player Mary Pierce, the genius of Glenn Gould and of Michael J. Fox, the greatness of mathematician S. S. Shrikhande, and love. He liked talking about love. He was a great ponderer of love, a thinker of feelings, a wanderer in the relationship jungle . . . and he liked marathoning on the phone about it. He had studied intimacy from every angle, it seemed, and had reached a few important conclusions about life and love—namely that marriage was a very bad thing and women needed to be rescued from it.

There was a six-foot blond heiress with a silver Lotus Elan who was rescued and became his steady girlfriend for many years. There was a dark, ephemeral beauty, a computer programmer, who was also rescued and became one of the rare women allowed to move into his house. There was also a former Chanel model whose marriage to an aristocrat had gone south. And there was Madame X, whose husband was so rich she simply refused to be rescued no matter what (a devastating blow).

It wasn't *stealing* women, exactly; it had more sense of mission than that. He was leading them to liberation and a kind of enlightenment. Dad imagined himself as some kind of one-man empowering machine, spending hours on the phone with his loves, offering advice and counsel, helping them extract themselves, helping them to be brave. When a relationship wasn't working and growing—anybody's relationship—he was quick to suggest it was time to move on. "It's like a plant in a pot," he told me as I sat on the edge of his bed, despondent over the end of a brief marriage to a man he had called the Plainclothes Jesuit, and later, when I was troubled over the termination of a long romance with Caveman Lawyer. "A relationship outgrows the pot you first plant it in, and eventually the two of you will decide to refigure it. All relationships need to be overhauled from time to time and allowed to change. You have to replant them. And at some point you'll need to repot, and one of you won't have the energy. That's when it's time to pull the plug."

I called him at the end of my relationships the way other women might call their girlfriends. He gave better advice. He gave advice that was so good that people still thank me for sharing it with them. Endlessly fascinated by breakups, he asked pertinent questions, seemed pleased to mull over the day-to-day sufferings and sorrows and second thoughts, and laughed with me over recriminations. It was a bit funny because, in general, Dad wasn't a very good listener. When it came to romance, though, he grew very quiet and soaked up every word as though he were processing information in order to issue a final readout. (For many years, he made his living as an expert in public-opinion polling.) And when a love affair ended, his advice was this: "You have to let yourself feel bad. You have to sit around and cry, preferably with the person you are leaving. You cry and cry and grieve the ending, the parting, and honor how all great passion will eventually dwindle into haze."

At the memorial service, his ex-girlfriends came alone—without the men they'd settled down with or married. Eight of them assembled themselves on his brown corduroy sofa for a group photo, arms around one another, laughing. There wasn't an ex-wife in sight. My mother, who had the terrible misfortune of marrying this fabulous man, sent flowers.

There were never any pictures of my brother and me in his bachelor apartments, and, later, there were none in his stark bachelor house in North Beach (there were four floors rising to a crow's nest, and only one bedroom—his) or in that last house on Wolfback Ridge. Marriage was the one grand and noticeable failure of his life, and it still hung around him like a shadow.

He once told me that, if he had to do it all over again, he wouldn't have had us, my brother and me. He liked to be shocking sometimes, more than truthful. I was quick to question him. "You wouldn't want to have me and Nathaniel?" I asked him.

"I'd want to have people like you in my life," he said, backpedaling. "But I wouldn't necessarily want you as my children."

I knew where he was going with this. It was hard being a good father when you weren't a good husband. The way the world is set up, the good husband—that Ozzie Nelson good guy, the domesticated man with sweater-vests and Labrador retriever sex appeal—is also the good father. And it was this sort of man and that sort of world that my father fled in 1966 when he left the suburbs of Glendale, California, where he and my mother had recently landed. He had tried hard, maybe even tried his best, but he had trouble being anybody but himself—the sort of father who swam in the pool wearing his sunglasses, who picked us up at the beach once dressed as the Invisible Man: a hat, gloves, turtleneck, and his face wrapped in Ace bandages.

He didn't watch sports. He played flamenco guitar alone in the living room after dinner and painted until the middle of the night. He disdained convention and enjoyed being rebellious. He shunned station wagons and even cars with backseats, opting instead for a 1953 white Corvette. And one afternoon toward the end of the marriage, when there was fifty dollars in the bank, he showed up with a new Triumph motorcycle. When my mother announced that we weren't allowed to ride with him, he bought little helmets for my brother and me and kept them hidden in the basement.

He needed to go away, "to get my doctorate at Stanford," he said finally. The truth was, he left us to become the theatrical figure that he was always meant to be, I guess, or the combination of people that he saw in himself. The bohemian, the academic, the urbane aesthete, and the bachelor who smoked very good dope and haunted nightclubs and drove a motorcycle around his North Beach neighborhood. Throughout the divorce, he sent letters to my mother, continuing to explain. "I dig the kids," he wrote. "I really do." But he never needed to explain it to me, although he kept trying. After he left, he was happier, freer, taller, and his back stopped going out. He fashioned a person out of his dreams and, I think, a better father for us—James Bond and Atticus Finch and Lawrence of Arabia all rolled into one.

It helped that he looked like a movie star. After he was gone, a friend of mine said, "Knowing your father was as close as I'll ever come to meeting Cary Grant." But he was never that physical or athletic or even masculine. He was six foot four and willowy . . . vaguely brooding and vaguely fey, a man who crossed his long stork legs the way Jeremy Irons might. When he was young, his hair was blue black and his face was long, his features open, his manner affected and austere. "Your father is the most handsome man I've ever seen," his own mother told me, "and also the most selfish." As a child, I watched the mothers of my young friends stumble over words while they spoke to him. Later, I watched my high school girlfriends and college roommates develop crushes on him—and wind up with innocent nicknames of their own. There were various phases of his perfect wardrobe—bell-bottoms gave way to straight-leg jeans, black leather was replaced by shearling, his dark blue three-piece suits became tweed. His hair turned whiter and whiter. In the last few years, he had a ponytail held back with a thin rubber band and he looked like Thomas Jefferson. And at the grand finale, stretched out in bed with his hands crossed over his chest, he still looked so good—so haunted and wistful, so Heathcliff—that I found myself gasping in surprise: "Look at you, Dad. You're still so goddamned beautiful, and *you're dead*." I quite loved him, quite adored him, quite worshiped him. Most of us women did, except maybe the two he married.

After he left my mother, he would never marry again. And he would never have more children. "I married a glamorous opera star," he often said, "and she wanted to be a housewife." It was a way of life that was abhorrent to him—an abhorrence that he was vocal about, usually in epithets. He could be harsh, tyrannical, opinionated—and a dreadful snob. And, maybe like all parents, he never stopped wishing that his children were more like him. It would have been a way to know, finally, that we approved of him, that we understood and chose to carry on the new family tradition of self-indulgence. There would be sports cars and motorcycles, Rolex watches, baby grand pianos, and rare guitars. There would be large renovation projects on very modern houses that we couldn't quite afford. There would be a bottle of Veuve Clicquot in the refrigerator at all times. There would be black limousines driven by out-of-work lute players. There would be roach clips fashioned from sterling silver and pre-Columbian beads. There would be a need for plastic surgery, calisthenics, recreational prescription drugs, a fish poacher, and triple-X-movie capabilities on the satellite dish. And there would be very effective birth control and a trail of former loves as long as the road behind us, each more wonderful and loving and exotic and accomplished than the last, none of whom had ever possessed us entirely.

"I like being a public temptation," my father used to say. "Don't you?"

He was always vaguely horrified by my instinct for settling into cozy houses and comfortable relationships and by my considering marriage. And I was always vaguely horrified by the way he asked how sex was with my boyfriends and by the Egon Schiele nudes with armpit hair on the walls in his bedroom. He wondered aloud why I wasn't interested in older men—"But Martha, twenty years is the perfect age difference!"—and I always fretted that one of my girlfriends would become one of his, although it was my brother, instead, who became quite accomplished at that. But as the years passed and I grew older and went on to have my own grand failures, I came to respect him and his world. And he came to respect mine. I stopped being embarrassed by him—by his anachronistic use of the word *balling* and by the John Altoon pastel of a naked woman with a green frog hopping out of her crotch that hung in the foyer. And eventually, Dad stopped lobbying me to remain single for the rest of my life. For one thing, he seemed to like somebody I was seeing—he called him Harvard—but perhaps there was a more pressing reason: with his death so imminent, he wanted to make sure I had someone to talk to after he was gone. "I've tried to hang on long enough," he told me during his last year, "to make sure you and your brother were looked after."

\ \ \

There were a lot of women to meet after he died. Neighbor Friend turned up at his memorial service—how she'd learned about it I'll never know—and found me right away. "I loved your father," she said. Her eyes were large and wet. Her overbite was hanging there like a theater balcony. A line of beautiful young girls from his office stood in the front row of the service with shaky lower lips and balled-up tissues. "He was my guardian angel," one sweet blond said. "Your father really helped me through some things," said another, vaguely. "He made me feel good about myself."

Another girl told me about how down-to-earth my father was, about how he'd talk to anybody as an equal. (This was news to me.) She told me a story about a new receptionist who was hired while Dad was sick and who, after a few months, asked, "Who is that very tall, distinguished man with the silver hair? He always comes and talks to me about my life."

"That's Peter Sherrill," she was told. "He owns the company."

"Don't tell me which girl is the receptionist," I said, looking around for a pretty face. "I should be able to point her out."

Mostly his buddies spoke at the service—his best friend from the Naval Academy, his fellow academics, a ballet director, his old boss, his partner in the software business he'd started in the last decade of his life, and my brother. ("I'm the only son of Peter Sherrill . . . as far as I know.") His art dealer read a Rilke poem. Another woman, an old colleague of Dad's, got up and spoke. She'd met my father in the early seventies, she said. He came into her office and the first thing he said to her, after an introduction, was, "I hear you're into women." She was a bit stunned and didn't know what to say. "Don't worry," my father said. "I am, too."

There were lots of love letters to paw through after he died. And a few movies to pay for—*Girls! Girls! Girls!*—that he'd watched off the satellite dish during his final days. A list of names was discovered, too—his loves, in order of appearance—with asterisks by certain names and underlining and other special marks that my brother and I were never able to decode. I have the list still, in my attic. And I have the letters, too, none of which I've been able to read. More came my way just a few months ago. Blue Icon sent me a shoe box of them, along with two framed photos he had sent her of himself. Her letters sat in my office in the shoe box until recently, when I was thinking about Dad and wanted something new, something that might feel almost alive, to have of him.

The letters to Icon are simple, wise, and full of bravado ("Until the lung cancer ten years ago, I was a statue") and charm ("Have you grown tired of my all-encompassing narcissism yet?"). In the letters, he reminds me again that he understood women. He knew how to talk to us, cheer us up, make us feel good. He was generous, sweet—and baroque. "If this paper could burst into flames in your hands and its ink etch your fingers and its printed words become sounds in your ears!" he writes to her. "Then I could have spoken to you like a distant magical song. And you, the unreachable, would finally be touched."

Sometimes he calls her Blue Eyes and sometimes Zelda and La Crantia and sometimes just Icon or Barbara. She calls him Ego.

He tells her that he has lived through "light despair" in his life and that he's come to enjoy a feeling he calls "the beautiful sadness." Many years have passed, and there have been many women, he confesses, but "I cannot think of a grander missed opportunity than you."

My life was always full of his women. And now that he's gone, I have some of his things—some books and furniture, the piano, the Glenn Gould CDs, and the fish poacher. My brother and I have decided to sell on the Internet the John Altoon drawing that we call *Frog Lady,* but we've found we can't part with the Schiele nudes. There's a skinny girl with armpit hair and thigh-highs on the wall of my office. And I have the letters in the attic, too, and I have his girlfriends, of course. My father bequeathed them to me after he died, tossing them like fading rose petals at my feet. They still call. They sent wedding presents when Harvard and I married and baby clothes when our son was born. They e-mail me jokes. They drop by when they're in town.

Icon and I are friends now, too, even though I've never seen her. She sent me a strand of antique beads after my father died. The necklace came in a fabric pouch with a card that just said, "Barbara." But I knew what the necklace was and why she'd sent it. He had given her a gift—and maybe the beads were part of it—and now she was passing it on to me. I think I know how she feels.

ABOUT THE CONTRIBUTORS

//

TOM CHIARELLA (1961-) is a writer-at-large for *Esquire*. He teaches writing at DePauw University in Greencastle, Indiana, where he still rides herd over his two sons, Gus and Walt.

LARRY DOYLE (1958-) is a former writer for *The Simpsons* and author of *I Love You, Beth Cooper*. His writing has appeared in *Esquire*, *The New Yorker* and *New York* magazine.

CAL FUSSMAN (1956-) was born in Brooklyn, New York, and traveled around the world before joining *Esquire* in 1997. He is the father of three.

TOM JUNOD (1958-) has won two National Magazine Awards for feature writing. He has been an *Esquire* writer-at-large since 1997.

JAKE LAMOTTA (1921-) is a former boxing world champion best known as the inspiration for the film *Raging Bull*. LaMotta was elected to the Boxing Hall of Fame in 1985 for winning 83 out of his 106 career matches.

SCOTT RAAB (1952-) is a graduate of the Iowa Writers' Workshop. He has been an *Esquire* writer-at-large since 1997.

RON REAGAN (1958-), the son of President Ronald Reagan, was quite fond of his father despite their political differences. He currently hosts a nationally syndicated daily radio program for Air America.

JOHN H. RICHARDSON (1954-) is an *Esquire* writer-at-large and has been writing for the magazine since 1997. His books include *In the Little World: A True Story of Dwarfs, Love, and Trouble*, and *My Father the Spy: An Investigative Memoir*. He's married to Katherine Potter and father to two beautiful and talented daughters, Julia and Rachel.

DAVID SEDARIS (1956-) is the author of *When You Are Engulfed in Flames, Dress Your Family in Corduroy and Denim, Me Talk Pretty One Day, Holidays on Ice, Naked*, and *Barrel Fever*.

MARTHA SHERRILL'S (1958-) books include *Dog Man, The Ruins of California*, and *The Buddha from Brooklyn*. Her writing has appeared in *Esquire, Vanity Fair*, and the *Washington Post*.

DANIEL VOLL'S (1970-) short stories have appeared in many periodicals. He is an *Esquire* contributing editor and an executive producer and writer of the television show, *The Unit*.

ALEC WILKINSON (1952-) is the author of nine books, including *Big Sugar, A Violent Act*, and *The Protest Singer*. He and his wife and son live in New York City.

INDEX

165

INDEX

Cover and Interior Design by Jon Chaiet

Library of Congress Cataloging-in-Publication Data

Fathers & sons : 12 great writers talk about their dads, their boys, and what it means to be a man / edited by David Katz. -- 1st pbk. ed.

p. cm.

Includes index.

ISBN 978-1-58816-805-4

1. Fathers and sons--Literary collections. 2. Fathers--Literary collections. 3. Fatherhood--Literary collections. I. Katz, David, 1975- II. Title: Fathers and sons.

PS509.F34F378 2010

810.8'035251--dc22

2009043964

10 9 8 7 6 5 4 3 2 1

Published by Hearst Books

A division of Sterling Publishing Co., Inc.

387 Park Avenue South, New York, NY 10016

Esquire is a registered trademark of Hearst Communications, Inc.

www.esquire.com

For information about custom editions, special sales, premium and corporate

purchases, please contact Sterling Special Sales Department at 800-805-5489

or specialsales@sterlingpublishing.com.

Distributed in Canada by Sterling Publishing

c/o Canadian Manda Group, 165 Dufferin Street

Toronto, Ontario, Canada M6K 3H6

Distributed in Australia by Capricorn Link (Australia) Pty. Ltd.

P.O. Box 704, Windsor, NSW 2756 Australia

Printed in USA

Sterling ISBN 978-1-58816-805-4